Getting Started

with *Vocal Improvisation*

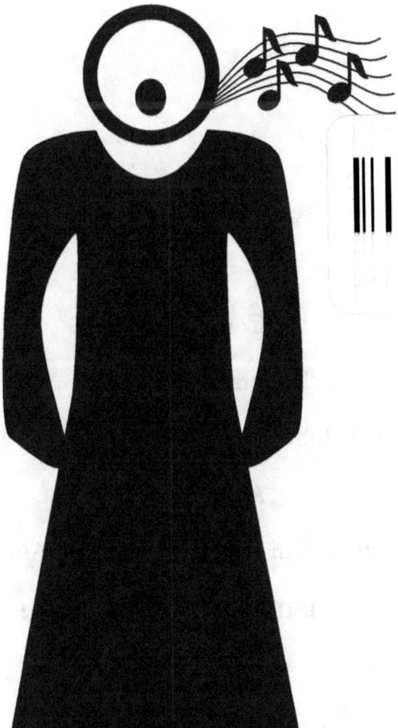

Patrice D. Madura

The National Association for Music Education

Copyright © 1999

MENC—The National Association for Music Education

1806 Robert Fulton Drive, VA 20191-4348

All rights reserved.

Printed in the United States of America

ISBN 13: 978-1-56545-116-2

Contents

Preface v

1. Why Teach Vocal Improvisation? 1

2. Freeing the Voice 5

3. Even Children Can Improvise 9

4. Popular Music, Gospel, and Blues Improvisation 21

5. Swing, Scat, and Authentic Vocal Jazz Improvisation 29

6. Classical Choral Improvisation 39

7. World Music Improvisation 51

8. Can and Should We Assess Vocal Improvisation? 59

References 63

Acknowledgments 66

Preface

Improvisation is a skill that most musicians would like to possess. It is often said that to be a complete musician, one must be able to improvise. The National Standards for Music Education, published in *National Standards for Arts Education* (1994), imply that all music teachers should be able to teach improvisation to K–12 students. Yet improvisation is one musical skill in which most of us have had little or no training. How can we be expected to teach musical improvisation if we have never improvised ourselves?

This book will address methods of teaching beginning vocal improvisation to K–12 students in the general music classroom and the choral rehearsal. These methods present beginning vocal improvisation as a skill that anyone can do, given a safe and supportive environment, a spirit of play, and a structured framework for the improvisational experience.

Whether you are looking for ideas on free improvisation with nontraditional sounds, ways to incorporate improvisation a la Kodály, Orff, or Gordon methodology into your general music curriculum, or strategies for teaching authentic improvisation in the vocal jazz rehearsal, the secondary choral rehearsal, or the world music class, I hope this book will serve as a valuable resource and confidence builder. Allowing ourselves and our students to participate in the creative activity of vocal improvisation will strengthen musicianship and encourage freedom of expression.

Chapter 1

Why Teach Vocal Improvisation?

Vocal improvisation has a long history; in fact, it is as old as music itself (Ferand, 1961). Before written notation existed, there was continuous reworking and embellishing of known vocal tunes. In many cultures a singer was criticized if he performed a song without embellishment or even if he sang a particular ornamentation more than once.

Vocal improvisation was certainly evident in early Christian music and continued through to the eighteenth century, at which time the practice of vocal ornamentation was taught systematically. Although the preference for technical agility over improvisation skill took place in the nineteenth century, renewed interest in improvisation emerged in the twentieth century with the introduction of jazz and the avant-garde movement.

This new interest in improvisation was reflected in several vital music education reform movements in the 1960s, such as the Tanglewood Symposium, the Manhattanville Music Curriculum Project (MMCP), and the Contemporary Music Project for Creativity in Music Education (CMP). *National Standards for Arts Education* (1994) was written as a result of the Goals 2000 congressional mandate, which proclaimed that arts education is a core curricular subject and emphasized the importance of improvisation (Mark, 1996). In all likelihood, the twenty-first century will be one that sees vocal improvisation as a vital musical activity in grades K–12.

Musical Rationale

Improvisation is much more than randomly making up music as one goes along. It is a "fundamental means by which musicians learn to coordinate ear, eye, and imagination and to perform what they hear in their minds" (McPherson, 1994, p. 161). Students enjoy creating and improvising music. The process of changing and interacting with musical materials according to individual choices gives personal meaning to the experience. This need to express oneself aesthetically can be a motivator throughout one's musical development. In fact, it has been found that students who participate in improvisation activities tend to continue musical activity as adults (McPherson, 1994).

Therefore, if K–12 music programs provided greater opportunities for creative musical experiences such as improvisation, more students from varied backgrounds might choose to become involved in music classes. Our profession must be willing to adapt to changing student needs.

Educational Rationale

Currently, the main motivator for learning to teach vocal improvisation is the National Standards for Music Education, published in *National Standards for Arts Education* (1994), which has strongly influenced the K–12 music curriculum framework of most of the United States (*The State of the Standards,* 1997). Content Standard 3 calls for all students to be capable of "improvising melodies, variations, and accompaniments" (*National Standards for Arts Education,* 1994, p. 27). Specific achievement standards for grades K–4, 5–8, and 9–12 describe how students are to demonstrate mastery of the content standard of improvisation. Specifically, by the time students have completed the fourth grade, they should be able to:

- "improvise 'answers' in the same style to given rhythmic and melodic phrases"
- "improvise simple rhythmic and melodic ostinato accompaniments"
- "improvise simple rhythmic variations and simple melodic embellishments on familiar melodies"
- "improvise short songs and instrumental pieces, using a variety of sound sources, including traditional sounds, nontraditional sounds available in the classroom, body sounds, and sounds produced by electronic means" (*National Standards for Arts Education,* 1994, p. 27).

By the time students have completed grade eight, they should be able to:

- "improvise simple harmonic accompaniments"
- "improvise melodic embellishments and simple rhythmic and melodic variations on given pentatonic melodies and melodies in major keys"
- "improvise short melodies, unaccompanied and over given rhythmic accompaniments, each in a consistent style, meter, and tonality" (*National Standards for Arts Education,* 1994, p. 43).

And, by the time students graduate from high school, they should be able to:

- "improvise stylistically appropriate harmonizing parts"
- "improvise rhythmic and melodic variations on given pentatonic melodies and melodies in major and minor keys"
- "improvise original melodies over given chord progressions, each in a consistent style, meter, and tonality" (*National Standards for Arts Education,* 1994, p. 60).

In addition, at the advanced level, high school students should also be able to:

- "improvise stylistically appropriate harmonizing parts in a variety of styles"

- "improvise original melodies in a variety of styles, over given chord progressions, each in a consistent style, meter, and tonality" (*National Standards for Arts Education,* 1994, p. 60).

Learning Theory

Students learn to improvise music in a series of stages, depending on their age, their previous musical experiences, and their technical facility (Konowitz, 1973; Kratus, 1991; Swanwick & Tillman, 1986; Thompson, 1980). Children develop their improvisation skills through an initial exploratory stage, where they freely experiment with sounds. This is followed by a structural stage, where they learn musical syntax and phrasing. Eventually, they reach a stylistic stage, where they learn the particular language of a style such as gospel, jazz, Baroque, or Indian raga. These three basic stages of improvisation learning—exploratory, structural, and stylistic—serve as the framework for this book.

Vocal improvisation has history, learning theory, and congressional impetus on its side. All it takes are curious and willing music educators to accept the task. Don't be another music teacher who "teaches as he or she has been taught" with regard to the study of vocal improvisation. Why not break the mold and have a lot of fun in the process?

Chapter 2

Freeing the Voice

Free vocal improvisation is something everyone can do. No special equipment is needed, and no knowledge of instrument technique is required. Everyone has a voice, and free improvisation works well in large classes. Free improvisation is about exploring sound possibilities without the constraints of traditional music rules of meter, tonality, or harmony. It is about discovering expressive ways to use the voice for speaking and singing.

Because exploring free vocal expression involves creating unusual sounds with the voice, there can be a risk of personal embarrassment or rejection. But because risk-taking is essential to musical creativity, the teacher must be sure that students feel safe to express themselves without fear of ridicule from other students. A safe and supportive environment that also includes a sense of play enables students to feel that their expressive efforts are respected and encouraged. Fear is the enemy of improvisation: it stops the creative impulse. Therefore, the teacher must find ways to create a comfortable environment, which may mean dimming the lights, having the students stand is a circle holding hands, or simply asking students to just smile, relax, and listen.

In the National Standards for Music Education, Content Standard 3d for grades K–4 can be accomplished with the activities in this chapter. This standard recommends that vocal students be able to "improvise short songs...using a variety of sound sources, including traditional sounds, nontraditional sounds...[and] body sounds" (*National Standards for Arts Education*, 1994, p. 27). However, students of any age can benefit from vocal exploration as preparation for more complex improvisation experiences later.

Motivation

How can we interest students in free vocal improvisation? Just listen to any recording by Bobby McFerrin to hear how many sound possibilities the human voice is capable of producing. His extreme uses of range, timbre, and imitation of musical instruments, coupled with perfect pitch and expression, provide a superb model to interest students in free vocal expression. The joy that McFerrin expresses as he sings is contagious, and it can provide further motivation for students to experiment with their voices, encouraging them to risk creating new sounds because it sounds like so much fun.

Free Improvisation Games

Many young children enter school with no knowledge of the expressive capabilities of the voice. They often need the teacher to help them explore the differences between their speaking voice and their singing voice, their whispering voice and their shouting voice, and their high voice and their low voice. Teachers can ask the children to echo them when they sing, "This is my high voice," or "This is my soft voice," to help them identify these different sounds. Later, individual children may improvise a call, using any vocal sound they find interesting, to be echoed by the rest of the class.

A traditional rhyme, such as "One, Two, Buckle My Shoe," can be used in beginning vocal improvisation, with one student improvising dynamics or vocal timbre (e.g., speaking, singing, whispering, shouting) for the numbers in the rhyme, while the rest of the class imitates that sound for the rest of the rhyme. The teacher should always model a few examples before the students are asked to try a new improvisation exercise.

Children enjoy improvising sounds to accompany movements. For example, one student might create a movement meant to represent swimming, while another would improvise water sounds with his or her voice. Or a movement representing cleaning a window could be accompanied by rubbing, squeaking sounds made by the voice, or students could combine the motions of flying a kite with sounds imitating the wind.

Improvising animal sounds may accompany the making of animal masks or other art work. Children can create the animal sounds that correspond to their particular masks, and then they can trade masks and explore other possible sounds for each animal. Children can also listen to Saint-Saens's *The Carnival of the Animals* and improvise animal movements to accompany the animal sounds they hear. Afterwards, it is important to have children discuss the most interesting improvised sounds and movements, perhaps after listening to a recording of the class improvisation.

The possibilities are endless for situations that can motivate vocal improvisation. The class can improvise group "soundscapes," such as a rainstorm, a beach scene, a crowded freeway, or popcorn popping. Visual aids can inspire class improvisation: a haiku poem, a teacher-created abstract map, real maps (e.g., of the school campus or the continent of Africa), or a painting by Monet or Picasso. Again, students should be encouraged to reflect on and discuss those improvisations that they consider to be the most effective and interesting and the reasons why. It is completely acceptable to re-create an improvisation based on students' feedback. Improvisation does not have to be completely spontaneous—reflective thought can be just as productive.

Group improvisation might focus only on the sounds of others' voices. Any vocal sound is acceptable as long as students are listening to the whole group or to individuals within the group. Students may enter and exit the group improvisation at any time, feeling free to participate only when they feel they have "something to say." They also can be encouraged to try to "make contact" with another singer vocally, by imitating that person's sound. (This improvisation is most effective with the lights dimmed or eyes closed, to eliminate visual distractions.) This group improvisation may last as long as it is interesting for the vocalists and may be allowed to fade out naturally.

The quintessential classroom resource for exploratory improvisation ideas is *The Thinking Ear* (1988) by R. Murray Schafer. The section titled "When Words Sing" is particularly valuable for its vocal improvisation suggestions, which can be applied successfully to any age, from kindergarten through college. Some favorite Schafer lessons are summarized here:

- "Melisma" asks students to produce the highest sound of which they are capable or the softest sound, the smoothest sound, the roughest sound, the funniest sound, the saddest sound, or a boring sound. Then, they are asked to tape-record themselves individually and, when playing it back, to try to counterpoint the recorded sound with live sounds that are opposite of the recorded sounds.
- "Nature Concert" suggests that students tell a well-known story by means of sound effects alone. Then the other students are asked to guess the meaning of the story.
- "The Biography of the Alphabet" describes a word as "a bracelet of voice-charms," which explains that each letter of the alphabet has colorful "metaphors that unlock secrets," such as "B has bite. Combustive. Aggressive. The lips bang over it," and "L is watery, luscious, languid. Needs juice in the mouth to be spoken properly" (Schafer, 1988, p. 180). Students can explore the sounds of the letters in their own names.
- "Onomatopoeia" asks students to discover some "water-sounding words," some "metallic-sounding words," some "bumpy," "shaggy," and "syrupy" words (Schafer, 1988, p. 183).
- "Vowels" suggests that students sing their favorite songs but totally eliminate the consonants.
- "The Psychographic Curve of the Word's Soul" asks the student to consider the meaning of the word "Credo" ("I believe") and write down all of his or her beliefs and convictions. The student then improvises a melody and sings his or her credo. Then the class can listen to Bach's "Credo" in the *Mass in B Minor*.

The more one participates in free improvisation, the more enjoyable and expressive it becomes. Free improvisation represents a release from all of the correct expectations that surround us on a daily basis and gives us a chance to delight in an aural playground where we can do no wrong. However, training for young musicians must include the structure of music as well. For as Stravinsky said, "The more art is controlled, limited, worked over, the more it is free" (1970, p. 66).

Chapter 3

Even Children Can Improvise

Children naturally impose structure upon their improvisations as they develop musically. Melodic and rhythmic patterns marked by repetitions begin to appear. Tonality, phrases, and meter emerge as children absorb the musical vocabulary that they experience in and out of school (Swanwick & Tillman, 1986). This natural inclination to impose structure on creative expressions begins around the age of six and continues throughout the elementary school years.

The teacher's role in this developmental process is to introduce students to various structural aspects of music, such as tempo, meter, tonality, and form (Kratus, 1995) through vocal improvisation activities. This chapter will present ways in which teachers can enable their students to improvise vocally in musically structured ways, while fulfilling improvisation standards for grades K–4 and 5–8. This chapter will also provide links between vocal improvisation activities and existing methodologies for teaching elementary music (Kodály, Orff, Dalcroze, and Gordon), keeping the development of musicianship as the ultimate goal.

Content Standard 3a for grades K–4 states that students will be able to "improvise 'answers' in the same style to given rhythmic and melodic phrases" (*National Standards for Arts Education*, 1994, p. 27). Several question-and-answer activities that fulfill this standard are presented in this chapter. It should be noted, however, that children should be able to imitate phrases accurately before improvising, so that they develop refined aural skills and learn the musical vocabulary that provides improvisation possibilities. For as Suzuki (1983, p. 1) said, "Japanese children can all speak Japanese" by learning it through imitation first. Imitation of models is the first step to improvisation in any style of music, whether it be Western classical, gospel, jazz, or multicultural.

Grades K–4, Standard 3a: Question and Answer Phrases

Prepare students for musical question-and-answer improvisation by engaging them in a conversation. Ask a few individual students questions, such as, "How did you get to school today?" or "What did you have for breakfast today?" Ask students to try to fit their answers into the same number of beats as the questions, having the entire class count the number of beats together.

For example:

"How did you get to school today?"
  1   2   3   4

"I took the bus to school today."
 1   2   3   4

"Do you have any pets?"
  1   2   3

"I have two cats."
 1 2   3

The Improvisatory Web

After some practice with the above exercise, the students will be ready to engage in a musical improvisatory conversation, during which they manipulate the elements of music in their improvised answers. Give students a short spoken phrase, such as "Let's go swimming!" and then ask them to repeat the phrase while changing a musical element, such as dynamics, pitch level, tempo, or rhythm. Later, sing a short phrase of five or six pitches that the class can imitate. Give students a list of musical elements appropriate to their level and ask them to choose one element to manipulate. When a student improvises the new phrase, have the class imitate it. Then, let the next student choose another element to manipulate, sing the new phrase, and have the class imitate it, and so on (Kaschub, 1997). Depending on the age and level of the students, the following musical elements may be manipulated:

- vocal tone color—speaking, singing, whispering, shouting, weeping, laughing
- rhythm—tempo, duration, meter, accents, patterns, syncopation, rests, accelerando, ritardando
- melody—contour, range, ornamentation (e.g., neighbor tones, passing tones, trills, turns, slides), scale type, chord type (*Experiments in Musical Creativity*, 1966)
- expressive devices—dynamics or articulations (e.g., legato, staccato, marcato)

Students should try to improvise answers that are of equal length to the question. Students may count the number of beats in the question together and may also clap or step the beats together. Adding movement aids in the vocal improvisation process and helps develop coordination and a solid sense of pulse, which are critical in early music learning.

The Telephone Game

A variation on the Improvisatory Web exercise is to have students stand in a circle. Have one student create either a spoken or sung phrase. Moving around the circle in clockwise motion, have each student manipulate one musical element of the previous phrase. At the end of the circle, compare the original phrase with the resulting phrase. Identify the musical changes that occurred and ask students which changes they find the most interesting.

Grades K–4, Standard 3b: Vocal Ostinato

Rhythmic Ostinato

Simple rhythmic and melodic ostinato accompaniments can also be improvised vocally. Take any age-appropriate song that the students know and choose one measure that has a rhythm you would like to use as the ostinato. Half the class may chant the ostinato rhythm while the rest of the class sings the song (Marsh, 1970). To encourage cooperative learning, arrange children in pairs and have one student choose a different measure to use as a rhythmic ostinato, while the other student writes words to go with it. Give each duo a chance to chant their ostinato while the class sings the song and tries to identify the measure with that chosen rhythm. To create variations on the rhythmic ostinato, students may explore augmentation (doubling the length of each note to make one measure's rhythm last for two measures) and diminution (double-timing the rhythm, but not the song).

Melodic Ostinato

Melodic ostinato accompaniments for the voice must match the harmonies of the song. The simplest way to begin is to find songs with only one chord, such as "Hot Cross Buns," "Rain, Rain, Go Away," or "London's Burning!" Choose one measure of melody to be used as the vocal ostinato, using the original words or writing new ones. Try each measure of the melody as a vocal ostinato accompaniment to the song. Then let individuals improvise (selecting from all possibilities) an ostinato, while the class sings the song.

Grades K–4, Standard 3c: Embellishment of Familiar Melodies

Students enjoy improvising simple rhythmic variations and melodic embellishments on familiar melodies. However, the words of a song make improvising with the voice more complicated than with instruments alone. This can be especially problematic in rhythmic improvisation, because new words must be improvised to fit the new rhythm. Some simple exercises are suggested below.

Rhythmic Variations

Simple rhythmic variations on a familiar melody might include changes in tempo (including accelerando and ritardando), durations, and patterns, as well as the addition of accents and rests. More advanced students may be able to change the meter and add syncopation. Consider the song "Hop, Old Squirrel." Students might improvise the tempo to show the rest of the class how fast or slow the squirrel hops. Or the teacher can suggest that they take the rhythm of the phrase "Hop, Old Squirrel," and find ways to vary the rhythm and then use words to match, such as:

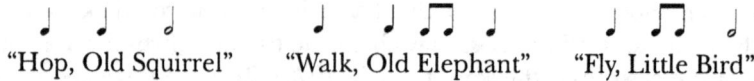

"Hop, Old Squirrel"   "Walk, Old Elephant"   "Fly, Little Bird"

In "Old MacDonald Had a Farm," students could improvise different animal names and their sounds to create different rhythms. For example, a cow goes "a moo moo here"; a hen goes "a cackle cackle here"; and a rabbit might go "a hoppity hoppity here." After a list is made of all possible animal sounds representing different rhythms, and after plenty of practice, each student may improvise a verse by calling out the name of the animal and singing the animal sound in rhythm, while the class claps that rhythm. Advanced students could improvise meter changes in "Scarborough Fair" or "Joyful, Joyful" from Beethoven's Symphony no. 9 by changing from duple to triple meter and back again.

Melodic Embellishments

Improvising melodic embellishments on familiar melodies can be taught easily in a number of ways. Students in grades K–4 can ornament the ends of song phrases with upper and lower neighbor tones. For example, in "Hot Cross Buns," they can ornament the pitch and rhythm of the word "buns" with an upper neighbor tone (UNT) and then return to the final note, changing the rhythm from a half note to two eighth notes and one quarter note. For example:

Have students try the same exercise with upper or lower neighbor tones (LNT) on "Hop, Old Squirrel." After they ornament these 3-note melodies and show that they know the difference between the original and the ornamented phrases, they can ornament phrase endings of other, more challenging melodies, using neighbor tones, anticipations (ANT), and appoggiaturas (APP), as in the following example of "Twinkle, Twinkle, Little Star":

Another simple melodic improvisation activity appropriate for students in grades K–4 can be done with any song having very simple rhythms and a very small vocal range. First, have students practice speaking its rhythm separately, using notation and "ta" and "ti-ti," or numbers, or whatever system you prefer. Then identify the pitches of the original melody and have students practice singing them in any order, while maintaining the original rhythm of the song. Try this with "Rain, Rain" or "Hot Cross Buns" and see how much fun this can be. This exercise helps your students develop good aural skills, especially pitch memory.

Grades 5–8, Standard 3a: Harmonic Ostinato

To vocally improvise simple harmonic ostinatos, students must be very familiar with the chord structure of the song, especially aurally. To begin, find songs that have only one chord, such as "London's Burning!" or "Row, Row, Row Your Boat." Play the tones of that chord for the students and provide ostinato models. The simplest ostinato might have only one pitch (e.g., do, mi, or sol) and one rhythm (e.g., all quarter notes). Ask students how they can make the ostinato more interesting (e.g., using more than one pitch and one rhythm). Let the class hear and explore all the possibilities within this limited scope. Then ask individuals to improvise an ostinato using any of the possibilities just explored. For example:

Words:	Row,	Row,	Merrily	Row
Beat:	1	2	3	4
Chord Tones:	do	sol	high do	sol

Later, add songs that have more chords, but be sure the chord sequence repeats throughout the song. An example is "Jamaica Farewell," which has four phrases, each containing four chords, one per measure: I, IV, V, I. First, have half the class sing the chord roots

while the other half sings the melody, and then switch parts. After students become secure with the chord roots as the harmonic basis of the song, they can learn to arpeggiate the chords: C-E-G, F-A-C, G-B-D, C-E-G. When half the class can sing the chord tones while the other half sings the melody, give students opportunities to improvise the following, while the rest of the class sings the melody.:
- Arpeggiate the chord, but change the rhythm.
- Change the order of the chord tones, but keep a steady beat.
- Change both the order of the chord tones and the rhythm (Hackett & Lindeman, 1997).

Words may be added to the ostinato:

Words:	Fare	thee	well,	Oh	Kingston	Town
Pitches:	C	C	G	G	F F	F
Chords:	I	-	-	-	IV -	-

Words:	Fare	thee	well,	Oh	Kingston	Town
Pitches:	G	G	B	B	C E	C
Chords:	V	-	-	-	I -	-

Grades 5–8, Standard 3b: Pentatonic and Major Variations

According to Standard 3b, vocal students should be able to "improvise melodic embellishments and simple rhythmic and melodic variations on given pentatonic melodies and melodies in major keys" by the time they complete grade eight (*National Standards for Arts Education*, 1994, p. 43). These lesson suggestions naturally follow those presented for grades K–4, where students embellished melodies but not in any specified tonality. Here, any simple pentatonic song or song in a major key that the students know well can be used.

For example, in the pentatonic song "I Gave My Love a Cherry," ends of phrases can be embellished with neighbor tones, anticipations, and appoggiaturas, just as was done in "Hot Cross Buns" and "Twinkle, Twinkle, Little Star" for grades K–4. Have the class sing the song, embellishing each phrase ending, first with upper neighbor tones, then anticipations, and then appoggiaturas. Then let individual students improvise phrase endings using one of the ornaments. Later, experiment with these ornaments in the middle of the phrases, particularly on the longer tones.

Songs in major keys are useful for teaching passing tone melodic variation. A song that uses mostly chord tones, such as "Skip to My Lou," can be ornamented with passing tones (PT) between the chord tones.

For example:

Or, melodies can be varied in the same way as described for grades K–4. Using a simple song in a major or pentatonic scale, isolate the rhythm with a system of rhythmic counting. Then, using all the pitch possibilities in the song (providing the notation will help), improvise new melodies to the original rhythm. Possible songs for this exercise include "Go Tell Aunt Rhody" and "Row, Row, Row Your Boat." As always in vocal improvisation, the challenge is in developing the "ear" or pitch memory well enough to stay in tune. While the instrumentalist can simply press keys, the vocalist must use the ear to produce the correct pitches, and these are excellent exercises for doing just that.

Students may improvise on their own compositions as well. Any of the pitches from the pentatonic scale can be used to compose melodies to Japanese haiku poems, and students may later improvise pentatonic variations on their own compositions. Haiku poems are always seventeen syllables long. Try these from *Cherry-Blossoms* (1960), or create your own:

- "That fat old bull-frog sat there staring back at me with a sour face."—Issa (p. 21)
- "Stubborn woodpecker...still hammering at twilight at that single spot."—Issa (p. 27)
- "Yellow butterfly...fluttering fluttering on over the ocean."—Shiki (p. 29)

Teaching Philosophies and Vocal Improvisation

Orff-Schulwerk

Improvisation is an integral part of the Orff-Schulwerk philosophy, and rhythmic improvisation is one of the primary goals of rhythmic experiences. Although rhythmic improvisation is often experienced through body percussion and instrument playing, it is learned first through rhythmic word games. This aspect of Orff-Schulwerk is of special importance to learning vocal improvisation.

Word Games. Short rhythmic patterns or beat subdivisions are selected, and children find words or names that fit them. For instance, the names "Kurt," "David," "Kimberly," and "Henrietta" fit the different subdivisions of a beat, as do the foods "plum," "apple," "ginger-snap," and "avocado." The children sit in a circle, patsching the pulse, and the game continues as long as words can be found to match the selected rhythm. Besides proper names and foods, other enjoyable categories for exploring rhythmic words are cars, cities, and vacation spots. Another way is to have the class chant a short phrase, such as, "Going shopping at the store; don't forget the _____ (quarter note or two eighth notes)," while each child improvises words that fit the rhythm.

Phrases and Form. Just as rhythmic units can be taught using words, larger aspects of form, such as phrases and sections, can also be taught though language. Well-known proverbs can be examples of short rhythmic phrases and meter, such as "Keep your own counsel," and longer phrases, such as "Count not your chickens before they are hatched." Rhymes are used to teach simple forms. Any of these may be used as a basis for vocal improvisation by having students improvise answers, changing the words and rhythm to respond to the teacher's musical questions (Warner, 1991).

Silent Reading. Improvisation activities are often used to reinforce newly learned music concepts, and children's improvisations show how well they have learned those concepts. For example, after teaching quarter notes, eighth notes, and half notes, write a four-measure rhythm exercise on the board, complete with words, but containing one blank measure. Ask the class to read the words in rhythm silently, filling in the empty measure with words that use any of the learned note values. Then have the entire class speak the exercise, simultaneously filling in the blank measure as each child chooses. Finally, give individuals the opportunity to perform solo, while the rest of the class identifies the rhythm of the words. Later, children may improvise entire answer phrases to question phrases, which can eventually lead to questions and answers in irregular meters such as 5/4 (Steen, 1992).

The Kodály Method

The Kodály Method is sometimes criticized for being rigidly focused on developing music reading, with little or no attention given to the creative activities of improvisation and composition. This is simply not true. The goal of the Kodály method is to integrate visual, kinesthetic, and aural (including improvisation) experiences for the purpose of developing the functionally literate musician. The literate musician should be able not only to read, but also to sing and write musical ideas. Choksy (1988) explains:

> At any time, the musical vocabulary with which children improvise... is always smaller than the vocabulary with which they can read and notate, and that, in turn is smaller still than the rote vocabulary. However, in all three of these levels—rote, reading-writing, and improvising-composing—creative activities can be a part of the music program. (p. 108)

At the rote level, new verses and movements may be created for songs that are beyond the musical reading and writing vocabulary. At the reading-writing level, musical questions and answers use new knowledge learned by the students to reinforce what they are being taught. Fluid improvisation using the new knowledge comes only after several months of repeated practice.

Because the Kodály method is based on singing, it is especially appropriate for the teaching of vocal improvisation in the schools. Below are improvisation guidelines for grades K–6 from Choksy's (1988) *The Kodály Method:*

- Grades K–1: Teachers and students playfully sing questions and answers to one another, using the solfège pitches of "sol," "la," and "mi." Later, the rhythms of "ta" (quarter note) and "ti-ti" (two eighth notes) are introduced.

- Grade 2: Rhythmic conversations should reinforce the learning of "ta" (quarter note), "ti- ti" (two eighth-notes), and "too" (half note). Answers should have the same number of beats as the questions. Four measure phrases of rhythm may include one empty measure that the student improvises. This leads to phrase forms of A–A–B–A, A–A–B–B, and A–B–A–C, where the teacher creates the "A" phrase and students improvise the "B" and "C" phrases. Next, the rondo form (A–B–A–C–A–D–A) may be introduced, in which the children compose "A" and perform it together as a class, while individual students improvise the other phrases. Melodic improvisation continues with question phrases sung by the teacher, ending on "re" or "sol" and the answer phrases, improvised by the children, ending on "do." They may improvise new words to known songs, as well.

- Grade 3: Children can continue to improvise new words and movements to known songs. Their rhythmic improvisations may include:

Melodic improvisations can include low "la" and low "sol" in question/answer phrases. Beginning harmonic ostinato improvisations can include measures taken from a song, with improvised rhythms and words.

- Grade 4: "Finish the Song" is an enjoyable game that requires the rote teaching of all but the last phrase of a song. Only the rhythm and the words of the last phrase are taught. Students finish the song by improvising their own melodies.

    In question and answer phrases, the teacher's questions should continue to include the newly learned pitches, and students should be encouraged to use the new pitches in their answers. Students use the same rhythm as the question and try to sing the teacher's last pitch ("re," "ti," or "sol"—the pitches of the V chord) to start the answer. Rhythms for improvisation at this level include:

- Grades 5–6: Students with several years of Kodály training are able to improvise at a high level of musicianship. These students should be able to vocally improvise by changing a known melody from major to minor; using sequences to extend melodic motives; augmenting and diminishing rhythms; using compound meters; accompanying with I and V, i and v, and i and V chords; using major scales and natural and harmonic minor scales; and using the following rhythms:

Dalcroze Eurhythmics

Although in Dalcroze Eurhythmics it is the piano, not the voice, that is the primary instrument of improvisation, it includes instruction that can be applied to teaching vocal improvisation as well. Here are a few suggestions from the appendix of Mead's *Dalcroze Eurhythmics in Today's Music Classroom* (1994, 203–204):

- "It is the doing that counts, not the finished product."
- "Have a musical idea before you start. Feel it in your...whole body. Hear it in your thinking ear."
- Always sing "what you hear...and hear what you" sing.
- "Once you begin [listening], follow [the tune], possessively, with your ear."

- "In the beginning, do not evaluate; just listen and assume a receptive attitude."
- "One usually uses too much material; your earliest efforts should be simple. Try to remember what you have [sung], and repeat it with a sense of purpose."
- "It is important to have contrasting material or contrasting sections."
- "Use silence to highlight something. Let your music breathe. Allow tense, dissonant, 'wrong places' to resolve naturally."

Gordon Audiation

Harmonic Improvisation Readiness Record (HIRR). Edwin Gordon (1996) claims that improvisation cannot be taught. He explains that "just as only a vocabulary of words, not thinking, can be taught, all a teacher can do is provide students with the necessary readiness to teach themselves how to improvise" (Gordon, 1996, p. 5). Fundamental to Gordon's music learning theory of audiation is learning a particular vocabulary of tonal, rhythmic, and harmonic patterns, which "provide readiness" for improvisation.

Gordon's *HIRR* (1996) has been designed for use with students in grades 3–12. His recommendations for teaching vocal improvisation to students with low scores on the *HIRR* include the following:
- Listen, sing, imitate, and improvise with a few simple, then later more complex, tonal and rhythmic patterns.
- Divide the class into three parts. Have the students sing the I–V7–I and I–IV–I chord progressions in close voicing and a comfortable key. Individual students can improvise melodic patterns at the same time.
- Have students sing the I–IV–V7–I and I–V7–IV–I progressions in close voicings, giving everyone the opportunity to sing all parts and to improvise a melody.
- Have students sing the I–IV–V7–I progression in harmonic minor.
- Have students listen to simple harmonic patterns played by harmonic instruments, both live and on recordings.

Improvisation Method. Gordon's new series, *Creativity in Improvisation* (1998), written with Azzara and Grunow, begins with the premise that the heart of improvisation is the learning of a large repertoire of tunes by ear, including their harmonic progressions. The books come with CDs for learning songs like "Long, Long Ago," "Mary Ann," and "Joshua," as well as tonal, rhythmic, and melodic patterns for improvisation on those tunes. Recorded accompaniments are also provided.

Singers should:
- listen to songs in a variety of meters and tonalities
- sing the tunes by ear, with and without words
- sing the bass lines of the tunes by ear
- sing tonal and rhythm patterns with syllables
- sing tonic and dominant functions in major and minor tonalities
- sing macrobeat, microbeat, and division functions in duple and triple meters

The goal of *Creativity in Improvisation*, as well as the majority of suggestions in this chapter, is to provide students with a vocabulary of songs, as well as tonal, rhythmic, and harmonic patterns, which are prerequisites to creating both intelligent and expressive improvisation.

Chapter 4
Popular Music, Gospel, and Blues Improvisation

After students have practiced free improvisation and learned to manipulate musical elements in structured improvisation, they are ready to learn to improvise in various styles, such as pop, gospel, jazz, or Baroque, each of which has its own musical syntax. Stylistic improvisation requires immersion in a particular style. Listening to and practicing vocal imitation of models in a particular style and studying their idiosyncrasies is recommended. In this and the next three chapters, ideas are presented for teaching stylistic improvisation, as specified in the National Standards for Music Education. (See the Gospel and Blues Discography sidebar on page 23 for artists and selections that can be used to teach this chapter in the classroom.)

Popular Music

To learn to improvise in a particular style, the best place to start is with vocal imitation of recorded examples. This process will help students learn to hear the particular vocal inflections, melodic embellishments, and rhythms that are characteristic of a style, and it will allow them to begin to incorporate that musical language into their personal musical vocabulary.

This learning technique is very effective for vocal improvisation in popular styles of music, such as bluegrass, ska, reggae, rap, Klezmer, and rock. For example, students can learn the bass line of a song in one of these styles by listening to a recording and imitating it. Once they can sing it in any octave, they can experiment with improvising simple musical elements, such as dynamics or timbre. Later, they can improvise by subdividing the rhythms into a limited number of beats or by adding one new pitch per phrase (Bitz, 1998).

Rap music can be helpful in teaching students to improvise various vocal timbres, syllables, and rhythms. Students can be guided to identify these various elements in a recorded rap song, imitate them, and then improvise their own raps using the same rhythms, timbres, and syllables. Students can work alone or in small groups to create an improvised rap (see Bitz, 1998, for rap discography).

Gospel

"Gospel music performance relies heavily on the vocal improvisation of the melodic line, and no two gospel music performances are ever the same" (Baker, 1983, p. 312). Gospel is a style that students may have been exposed to at home, in church, or through the media. In fact, those students who otherwise might not participate in a traditional choral group might be more inclined to join a gospel choir. For those students who are already familiar with the style of gospel music, learning vocal improvisation can strengthen their musicianship, especially their aural skills.

For gospel improvisation, any well-known spiritual can be used to start. Possibilities include "Amazing Grace," "He's Got the Whole World in His Hands," "Joshua Fought the Battle of Jericho," "O Happy Day," and "Michael, Row the Boat Ashore." The following techniques for improvising in the style of gospel music are suggested by Baker (1983), Cox (1995), and Smallwood (1980):

- Alter or embellish the original melody by adding blue notes (see next section, "The Blues"), upper and lower neighbor tones, passing tones, anticipations, octave displacement, large skips on particularly important words, bends (raising or lowering less than a semitone), and portamento.
- Alter the original rhythm by avoiding singing on the beats, by "worrying the note" (subdividing or repeating in a rapid and restless manner, leaving very little rhythmic space), and by adding syncopation.
- Alter the meter by changing from simple duple meter to a swinging meter of 12/8.
- Alter the lyrics by adding, repeating, or deleting text; using "lazy" diction; or using vocal stops (placing rests between words or syllables in words).
- Alter the cadences by delaying the final pitches of phrases and delaying the tonic through passing tone ornamentation.
- Alter the timbre by transferring life experiences into sound, using growls, screams, moans, hums, and cries, as well as vibrato and falsetto, to communicate conviction in the message.

One does not have to be of a particular ethnic group to teach gospel music. As in any style of music, the improviser (and teacher) must listen to recordings and live performances as models. Theoretical knowledge alone will not produce anything resembling an authentic style. Only extensive listening to and imitating of the masters, combined with the theoretical guidelines, will produce genuine results.

It is recommended that the teacher choose recordings that contain well-known songs, so that students can compare the original melodies with the recorded gospel versions, using the above list of techniques for altering a song in gospel style. Students should then try to imitate the improvisations and try some of their own.

The following list of gospel artists provides a starting point for aspiring students and teachers in the art of gospel improvisation: Yolanda Adams, Vanessa Bell Armstrong, Shirley Caesar, James Cleveland,

Darrel Coley, Sam Cooke, Andrae Crouch, David Sisters, Fisk Jubilee Singers, Edwin Hawkins, Walter Hawkins, Mahalia Jackson, Roberta Martin, Sanctified Singers, Don Shirley, Myrna Summers, "Sister" Rosetta Tharpe, Clara Ward, the Dark Woods Ensemble's *Soulful Messiah* (based on Handel's *Messiah*), and the soundtracks to *Sister Act II*, *The Preacher's Wife*, and *The Apostle* (see the sidebar discography for more details).

The Blues

Gospel and Blues Discography

The Blues: A Smithsonian Collection of Classic Blues Singers. 4 CDs. Smithsonian RB0001.
Boogie Woogie, Jump, and Kansas City. Folkways Jazz, vol. 10, 2810.
Cleveland, James. *James Cleveland and the Southern California Community Choir*. Savoy 14270.
Crouch, Andrae. *Pray*. Cassette, 1997. Warner Brothers 9 45924-4.
Fisk Jubilee Singers. Folkways FA 2372.
Franklin, Aretha. *Amazing Grace*. Atlantic SD 2906.
Franklin, Kirk. *Kirk Franklin and the Family Christmas*. Cassette, 1995. Gospo Centric INTC- 90209.
Gospel Songs of Thomas Dorsey. Columbia KG 32157.
Hawkins, Edwin. *Oh Happy Day*. Buddah 5086.
Jackson, Mahalia. *The Best of Mahalia Jackson*. Cassette, 1995. Columbia/Legacy CT 66911.
Jackson, Mahalia. *I Sing Because I'm Happy: Interview with Songs*. Cassette, 1992. Smithsonian Folkways SFSP90002.
Jackson, Mahalia. *In the Upper Room*. CD, 1997. Malaco SXCD 3117.
Johnson, James P. *The Original James P. Johnson*. CD. Smithsonian SF 40812.
Lewis, Meade Lux. *Barrel House Piano*. Archive of Folk and Jazz Music 268E.
Shirley, Don. *The Gospel According to Don Shirley*. Columbia CS 9723.
Smith, Bessie. *The Essential Bessie Smith*. 2 CDs, 1997. Columbia/Legacy C2K 64922.
Wow Gospel 1999: The Year's 30 Top Gospel Artists and Songs. 2 CDs, 1999. Zomba 01241- 43125-2.

While blues music is a style that is considered by some to be the secular form of gospel music, the link is based on the African-American origin, which creates similarities in vocal inflection and rhythmic feel. However, "the blues" has a specific chord progression, scale, and textual form, which gospel music does not. The blues progression, scale, and lyrics are simple, and thus an excellent vehicle for teaching beginning vocal jazz improvisation.

One way to begin teaching the twelve-bar blues is to play a recording and have students identify the form of the lyrics. If the selected song is a twelve-bar blues, the form of the lyrics is A–A–B, with the words of the first and second phrases identical, and the third phrase contrasting. This occurs during each verse or twelve-bar repetition. For instance:

A	My bed is hard and the weather outside is cold
A	My bed is hard and the weather outside is cold
B	I'd go to California but my car is wrecked and old
A	The alarm is ringin' but I don't want to go to school
A	The alarm is ringin' but I don't want to go to school
B	My mom says "Honey, if you don't, you'll be a fool!"

You can find excellent recorded examples of the twelve-bar blues by Bessie Smith, Ma Rainey, and Joe Williams. Carefully listen for the A–A–B form because some songs are titled "blues" but are atypical. In fact, a recent two-CD set by Bessie Smith, who has been named the "Empress of Blues," contains less than half twelve-bar blues songs. But it is easy to tell which ones are twelve-bar songs by listening for the A–A–B lyrics. (It is also recommended that the teacher listen to all recordings prior to playing them for the class to make sure the lyrics are appropriate. Many blues artists sing about drinking, gambling, and cheating on their women, and these recordings should certainly be carefully screened for classroom use. Bessie Smith is usually a good and safe choice.)

Students will easily recognize the A–A–B form of the lyrics, as well. They can be encouraged to sing along with the recording and then improvise their own blues lyrics to fit the recorded melody. After each student improvises his or her lyrics, the entire class can repeat those lyrics for one verse. Some students will prefer to write their lyrics as a homework assignment, which is acceptable, although they should be reminded that blues singers often improvise their lyrics on the spot and that the lyrics often reflect life's problems. As always, the teacher should model a few sample improvisations before asking the students to improvise on their own.

The basic chord progression of the twelve-bar blues is the following, with one chord per measure:

4/4	I	I	I	I
	IV	IV	I	I
	V	V	I	I

The following alteration is common:

4/4	I7	IV7	I7	I7
	IV7	IV7	I7	I7
	V7	IV7	I7	I7

Many other possibilities may emerge from these basic progressions and can become quite complicated, but both of these progressions are perfectly appropriate places to begin when teaching students about the blues.

The twelve-bar blues chord progression will sound familiar to everyone. It is a common progression that occurs in boogie-woogie, rock, and jazz, and students will feel comfortable with it quickly. All they need to do is learn the primary chords (I, IV, V) in one or two keys to get started. The piano keyboard is an excellent visual aid for learning the primary chords. Even upper elementary and middle school students can learn to play the twelve-bar blues in the key of C with a little practice. The instrumental experience of playing the blues is important, and all students should be able to memorize and play the progression. To make it enjoyable, the teacher or a student with piano skills should play a "walking" bass line (all quarter notes) or provide a recorded blues accompaniment, such as Jamey Aebersold's CD (1988), *Nothin' but Blues*.

Students should sing the roots to the chords while listening to recorded examples as the teacher points to the correct chord in the progression. Later, they should be able to sing the roots to the chords in the twelve-bar blues with no accompaniment at all. They may sing the roots on "loo" or solfège or numbers, whichever system the teacher prefers. But without knowing the harmonic structure of the blues completely, there is no way a student will progress in blues or jazz vocal improvisation, which will only become more complex. Knowing the harmonic progression is key. It is especially important for singers because they have no key to play that automatically puts them on the correct pitch, as do many instruments.

Recorded examples of twelve-bar blues progressions abound. The earliest clear examples for classroom use are the boogie-woogie and blues pianists such as Meade Lux Lewis, James P. Johnson, and Pete Johnson. The basic twelve-bar blues progression is easy to hear because it is played by the left hand of the pianist. Certainly, the early vocal blues are also good classroom models, especially when Bessie Smith is accompanied by Fletcher Henderson or Pete Johnson.

Students enjoy learning to sing boogie-woogie bass lines, and it is excellent aural training for them to sing the pattern of 1-3-5-6-flat7-6-5-3 in quarter notes on "doo" for each of the primary chords. When the group accomplishes this, challenge them further by dividing the class into four groups, having each group sing a chord tone (the root, third, fifth, and flat seventh) and the whole note chords in the twelve-bar blues progression. In addition, have individuals chant their A–A–B blues lyrics in time with the accompaniment, as a preparatory exercise to singing them later.

One aspect of teaching blues that remains elusive to many teachers is how to teach "swing." They may explain that in swing, two eighth notes are uneven and should be executed as a triplet with the first two notes tied together, such as:

♫ = ♩♪ (triplet)

But swing is not an intellectual matter. It is a physical phenomenon. Duke Ellington summed up this style in the title he gave to one of his most popular pieces, "It Don't Mean a Thing, If It Ain't Got That Swing."

The best way to teach swing is to play blues recordings in class that do swing. Then have everyone snap, clap, or tap on beats 2 and 4. Have them be as physical as they want—swing is not a subtle thing. Swing is visceral. It has to be felt with every fiber of the being. The teacher must model the feeling of swing while the students are listening to examples in class. Also, when students or the teacher play the blues chords or bass line on the piano, beats 2 and 4 should be slightly accented. (Swing is addressed in more detail in Chapter 5.)

The last element of the blues to be learned is the blues scale. The blues scale is made up of the following scale degrees: 1, flat 3, 4, flat 5, 5, flat 7, and 1. Thus, in the key of C, the blues scale is:

This is where it gets tricky for singers. It is much easier to play these notes on the piano than it is to sing them accurately.

The good news is that the blues scale stays the same when the chord changes. In other words, in the twelve-bar blues in C Major, the blues scale will work over the I chord (C), the IV chord (F), and the V chord (G). There is no need to change to an F blues scale or a G blues scale when the chords change.

The next step is to teach students the sounds of the blues scale. A good place to start is by modeling extremely simple melodies using one or two pitches from the blues scale to fit the A–A–B blues lyrics of previous class improvisations. Good, workable pitches are the 1, the flat 7, and the flat 3. Often, blues melodies begin on the high tonic and use the nearby flat 7 and flat 3 before descending through the blues scale. Repeated motives are frequent (Eskelin, 1994).

Experiment with different combinations of blues scale pitches to fit the lyrics and then try them out with the Aebersold (1988) *Nothin' but Blues* recorded accompaniment. Try other combinations, and practice, practice, practice until the blues scale begins to feel comfortable.

Chapter 5
Swing, Scat, and Authentic Vocal Jazz Improvisation

Have you considered teaching your vocal students how to improvise using scat singing? Think of the exhilarating singing of the late Ella Fitzgerald (1917–1996). Her fluid, improvised melodies are excellent models of scat singing for students of vocal jazz. Other successful vocalists such as Sarah Vaughan, Betty Carter, Anita O'Day, the late Mel Tormé, Jon Hendricks, and Bobby McFerrin have also developed their own personal styles of scat singing. (See the sidebar Vocal Jazz Discography sidebar for artists and selections that can be used to teach this chapter in the classroom.)

How can you guide your students in developing basic, but authentic, vocal improvisation skills? Studies suggest that to scat sing successfully, vocalists need five things:

- extensive exposure to jazz performances, both live and recorded, especially instrumental jazz;
- the ability to accurately imitate melodies and rhythms with the voice;
- some knowledge of jazz theory, both aural and written;
- dedication to practice; and
- willingness to use self-evaluation.

These five predictors of vocal jazz improvisation ability will be emphasized in strategies for teaching the authentic elements of jazz improvisation throughout this chapter (Madura, 1996).

What are the elements of an authentic vocal jazz improvisation? One need only listen to scat solos by Ella Fitzgerald, Mel Tormé, the New York Voices, or The Ritz to identify them. Some essential elements include:

- swing and jazz rhythms,
- scat syllables,
- jazz tonal language,
- standard jazz repertoire,
- rhythm section accompaniment (piano, bass, and drums),
- appropriate vocal tone quality,
- interaction between the singer and the instrumentalists, and
- originality.

Your students will need extensive experience with listening to and imitating jazz. Plan a little time during each rehearsal to listen to jazz recordings. Class assignments might include attending live jazz performances, listening to specific jazz recordings, and imitating short phrases from them. If students don't listen to jazz, they will neither understand the concept of an authentic jazz solo nor learn how to "swing."

Swing

The concept of "swing" is essential to scat singing and presents a challenge to students who have experienced only the straight eighth-note feel of most other music, including classical, rock, and Latin. The swing feel is best achieved through aural means, and, as stated in the previous chapter, students should be encouraged to snap the fingers or tap the foot on beats 2 and 4 while listening to swing recordings. As simple as this may sound, many novices to jazz have difficulty with this off-beat accentuation. An excellent recording to illustrate swing is *How Long Has This Been Going On?* on Fantasy Records, featuring Sarah Vaughan. Among other "hard-swinging" artists are the Count Basie Band, Oscar Peterson, Sonny Rollins, Ella Fitzgerald, and the Hi-Los.

To help train the ear, create one-measure calls for students to imitate, clapping the swinging eighth notes. Avoid the tendency to emphasize the notes that fall on the beat. The off-the-beat note should receive a very subtle accent, creating the propulsive, rhythmic flow known as swing. Then create call-and-response phrases that include other subdivisions of the beat and syncopations, as seen in this example:

Encourage students to clap improvised calls, using the swinging rhythmic patterns, while the rest of the class listens and imitates. They should continue to tap the foot on beats 2 and 4. Every student should have the opportunity to practice improvisation every day, even if it involves simple clapping of swing rhythms in the early stages of learning improvisation. They also should engage in group evaluation and self-evaluation by discussing those rhythmic improvisations that they found the most effective or interesting.

Scat

Scat syllables are directly related to jazz rhythmic phrasing and are derived from instrumental jazz articulations, especially those of horn players. They are not pure nonsense syllables, as many books suggest. Just listen to "Robbins' Nest" from *Ella and Basie!*, on Verve Records, where the Count Basie Band sounds like it is imitating Ella's scat syllables. Scat singing supposedly originated when Louis Armstrong forgot the words to a song and began singing trumpet-like syllables.

To sing authentic-sounding scat syllables, there are some simple guidelines that are especially helpful to the beginning vocal improvisor.

Sing "doo" on full-value eighth note downbeats, "bah" on full-value eighth note upbeats (or the middle eighth in triplets), and "dah" on full-value final eighth notes in triplets. For shorter values, sing "dit" on downbeats and "bop" on upbeats (Garcia, 1990), without pronouncing the "t" or "p," but rather, just stopping the air flow. Improvise calls for the students to imitate and then have each student practice improvising calls. Use this example:

doo-bah doo-bah doo-bah-dah doo-bah doo-bah doo-bah bah doo-bah dit doo-bah bop bop

The importance of rhythmic phrasing and the accompanying scat syllables cannot be overestimated in creating authentic vocal jazz improvisations. Even with correct pitch and harmony relationships and authentic jazz "licks," "riffs," and "quotes" (to be explained later), the improvisation will not sound like jazz if the rhythmic feel is not secure. Students should be encouraged to find an interesting scat solo, listen to it, and imitate (completely by ear or through written transcription) the rhythmic and scat phrasing of a portion of the solo, disregarding the pitches. The more students listen to and imitate scat solos, the sooner they will begin to internalize the jazz language. Later, they can perform the solo with the original pitches for the rest of the class.

Accessible scat solos can be found in Sarah Vaughan's "Shulie a Bop," on *Swingin' Easy* by Trip Records. A humorous example for the classroom that includes call-and-response that students can imitate is Bobby McFerrin's "I Hear Music" from *Spontaneous Inventions* on Capitol. Other notable scat singers include Louis Armstrong, Dizzy Gillespie, Betty Carter, Babs Gonzales, Clark Terry, Janet Lawson, Kevin Mahogany, the Double Six of Paris, and Lambert, Hendricks & Ross.

An excellent resource for expanding the scat vocabulary is Stoloff's exercise book and accompanying CD, *Scat! Vocal Improvisation Techniques* (1996), which includes both rhythmic and melodic scat-singing practice examples, including some that are particularly appropriate as vocal warm-ups for the vocal jazz rehearsal. For example, have the students sing a C major scale in thirds ("do-mi, re-fa, mi-sol, fa-la, sol-ti, la-do, ti-re, do; do-la, ti-sol, la-fa, sol-mi, fa-re, mi-do, re-ti, do") with swinging eighth notes and scat syllables (on "doo bah"). This warm-up can help develop vocal technique and jazz styling simultaneously. For variations, start at the top of the scale to help retain the head voice quality, increase the tempo to help develop vocal flexibility, or move the pattern up and down to develop vocal range. Develop similar warm-ups using pentatonic and blues scales, as well as Mixolydian and Dorian modes, perhaps first with solfège syllables and then with scat syllables.

Voice Quality

Vocal Jazz Discography

Fitzgerald, Ella. *The Complete Ella in Berlin: Mack the Knife.* CD, 1993. PolyGram 314 519 564-2.
Fitzgerald, Ella. *The Duke Ellington Songbook.* LP, 1980. Polydor
Fitzgerald, Ella. *Ella and Basie!* CD, 1997. Verve 314 539 059-2.
Fitzgerald, Ella. *Ella Fitzgerald at the Opera House.* CD, PolyGram 831269.
Hendricks, Jon. *Recorded Live at the Trident.* CD, 1991 PolyGram 314 510 601-2.
Hendricks, Jon and Friends. *Freddie Freeloader.* CD, 1990. A&M 81757 63024.
The Jazz Singers: A Smithsonian Collection. 5 CDs, 1998. Smithsonian RJ0040.
Jefferson, Eddie. *The Jazz Singer.* CD, 1993. Evidence 30182-20622.
Jefferson, Eddie. *The Main Man.* Cassette, 1981. Inner City TIC 1033.
King Pleasure Sings, Annie Ross Sings. Fantasy 7128.
Manhattan Transfer. *Vocalese.* Atlantic 7567-81266-4.
McFerrin, Bobby. *Play.* CD, 1992. Capitol 7777-95477-2.
McFerrin, Bobby. *Spontaneous Inventions.* Cassette, 1986. Capitol 4BT 85110.
McRae, Carmen. *Carmen Sings Monk.* CD. BMG 1241-63086-2.
New York Voices. Cassette, 1989. GRP 9589.
New York Voices. *Hearts of Fire.* CD, 1991. GRP 11105-9563-2.
The Ritz. CD, 1987. Denon 81757 1839 2.
Vaughan, Sarah. *How Long Has This Been Going On?* CD, 1987. Fantasy.
Vaughan, Sarah. *Swingin' Easy.* Cassette, 1978. Trip CA TLP 5551.
Williams, Joe; Hendricks, Jon; Lambert, Art; Ross, Annie. *Sing Along with Basie.* EMUS ES- 12004.

Certain vocal qualities and techniques are often associated with vocal jazz singing. These include straight-tone singing, breathiness, bright vowels, slides, fall-offs, and so on. Students should be encouraged to listen to various vocal jazz soloists and imitate those that they prefer. However, the vocal jazz teacher should make certain that the serious music students do not learn habits that may be detrimental to their future vocal development. There is a danger that students who sing only vocal jazz, and then later decide to become choral teachers, will be unable to demonstrate and teach the darker, more mature, and more vertical vowel sounds that classical choral music often requires. Another concern is that a conflict may occur between what the private voice teacher and the vocal jazz director request, in terms of vocal technique. In this area of vocal jazz, vocal health should be the prime concern. Keeping the lines of communication open with private teachers and/or university voice faculty should be a priority, as well, as doing so will benefit your students and your program. A good source for teaching vocal jazz techniques is Kirby Shaw's *Warm-ups for the Jazz/Show Choir* (1990), published by the University of Northern Colorado Jazz Press.

Jazz Tonal Language

The serious jazz student must learn the jazz tonal language, which consists of chord/scale relationships, "licks" (commonly used jazz patterns), "riffs" (repeated motives), "quotes" (brief melodic phrases taken from other melodies but substituted over the same chord sequence), chromaticism, and chord substitutions. Where does one begin to learn and assimilate the jazz tonal language? Given that a knowledge of jazz theory aids in the development of improvisation skills, start by teaching the spellings and sounds of jazz chord types (e.g., major, minor, dominant, half-diminished, fully diminished, and augmented) with the possible extensions (such as flat 9, sharp 9, sharp 11, and flat 13) and scale types (major, pentatonic, blues, Dorian, Mixolydian, Lydian, diminished, and whole-tone), as well as chord and scale relationships. A clear explanation of the scale options for any given chord is available in David Baker's (1988) *Jazz Improvisation* and Jamey Aebersold's (1988) improvisation CDs with accompanying texts.

Introduce improvisation skills to your students by including daily practice with the twelve-bar blues. Play as many examples of twelve-bar blues recordings as you can to help students internalize the sound of the basic chord progression. Have students memorize the basic blues progression (I7, I7, I7, I7, IV7, IV7, I7, I7, V7, IV7, I7, I7) and master singing the chord roots, first with recorded examples and later without recordings. A solid aural understanding of the underlying chord progression of a piece is critical to any jazz improvisation.

After students have learned to sing chord roots, teach them the blues scale: 1, flat 3, 4, flat 5, 5, flat 7, and 1. The blues scale is a horizontal scale, meaning that it can be sung in the tonic key of the blues, even when the chords change (see previous chapter for explanation). Students will often have a particularly difficult time singing a flat 3 over the major tonic chord, but it is the dissonance of the "blue note" (the flat 3) that should be emphasized and enjoyed.

The painless method is to provide a jazz play-along recording of rhythm section accompaniments, such as Aebersold's (1988) *Nothin' but Blues*, which provides the blues in every key. Choose a moderately slow track and have each singer improvise just one measure of it. To make it even easier, tell students to begin by singing only the first scale degree. Have them improvise rhythmically on the one note and make it "swing." Tell them that there is nothing a singer can do "wrong" in improvisation and have them experiment until they get comfortable. Next, tell students to add flat 7 to the first scale degree and improvise on just those two notes. Gradually have them add more pitches, measures, and scale options. Always keep a comfortable and supportive atmosphere. This process can take a long time, but daily practice and the incentive of having their improvisations featured in the school concerts will help your students progress.

Often jazz "riffs" are used to create an earthy feel to the blues. A riff is a repeated motive, as in this example:

The sheer repetition of a blues motive creates a groove that audiences find undeniably attractive at certain climax points.

Another delightful jazz practice is to "quote" another melody in an improvisation. For example, during "Blue Monk," a quote from another blues tune, such as "Tenor Madness," could occur over any appropriate chord. Or, the melody of any jazz tune that has a ii-V progression in it may be used to insert a quote from another tune (jazz or nonjazz) that has the same harmonic progression. The key to making quotes effective is to sneak them in briefly and unexpectedly among the rest of the improvisation. Quotes are often easily recognized by audience members and are usually greeted with knowing laughter and applause.

In the twelve-bar blues, there are other scales that are used for improvisation besides the blues scale. The Mixolydian scale tones (same as major but with a lowered 7th) can be sung over each chord. Students should practice by first singing the roots of the chords, then the triads, the seventh chords, and finally the whole of the Mixolydian scales.

For example:

Even more in the style of jazz would be the inclusion of a natural seven in each of the Mixolydian scales, resulting in the bebop scale, as in this example:

Note that the extra tone makes descending chord tones occur on strong beats, creating a more natural feel to the scalar line. The next example shows one of the first common bebop patterns, or "licks," that an improviser learns:

When improvising to the blues, the singer may use the blues scale, the Mixolydian scale, the bebop scale, riffs, licks, and quotes. Students can experiment to find the most effective ways to mix and match the possibilities.

It is possible to teach jazz improvisation without beginning with the blues, and some teachers prefer to do so. As stated earlier, the blues scale creates difficulty for singers at first, because the "blue 3rd" is sung against the major 3rd of the chord. An alternative approach would be to start beginning improvisation instruction with a modal or Dorian tune, where every note of the scale is consonant. For example, in a tune based on Cmin7 (ii7) chords, the student learns that the chord tones are the 2, 4, 6, and 8 of the BbMaj7 (I) chord. Call-and-response using chord tone patterns that swing is emphasized. Later, this method leads to improvising over the ii-V progression, which comprises 75 percent of jazz (Berg, 1998).

For more information on improvising over ii-V progressions, review the Mixolydian and bebop scales in this chapter. They may be used over any V7 chord, as well as that chord's ii. The reverse is also true—the Dorian scale of any ii chord can be used over its V. Actually, the parent scale of the ii-V progression is the major scale of the I (tonic) chord, but often in jazz, the ii-V progressions are brief and do not resolve to I. More than one hundred ii-V patterns used in the jazz language can be found in David Baker's (1986) *How to Play Bebop*.

Repertoire

It is often difficult to find repertoire that encourages vocal improvisation or that teaches the standard jazz selections. One excellent source for this kind of literature is the University of Northern Colorado Jazz Press. Choose vocal jazz literature that includes open sections for improvisation on familiar chord progressions, complete with chord symbols.

Standard jazz chord progressions include the twelve-bar blues, "rhythm changes" (the chord progression to Gershwin's "I've Got Rhythm"), and modal and ii-V7 progressions. The chord symbols not only inform the singers of the chord/scale relationships needed for improvisation, but keep the rhythm section players (piano, bass, and drums) motivated. Often these players come from the jazz band and want to play jazz because of its creative possibilities. They usually are not content to play only written accompaniments for the vocal jazz ensemble. Be sure to give them occasional improvisation solos, as well. They will enjoy "trading fours" with the singers or having a whole chorus to themselves for soloing.

Start by selecting one moderately easy blues piece, so that time can be spent practicing improvisation, rather than just learning difficult chord voicings (although a concert performance should ideally feature songs with difficult chord voicings, as well). Some examples of accessible blues arrangements that can be used as beginning improvisation vehicles include "Blue Monk," "Doodlin'," "Things Ain't What They Used to Be" (all arranged by Dave Cross), and "Tenor Madness" (by Michele Weir). "Everybody's Boppin'" (by Mark Mazur) is ideal for teaching rhythm changes. These arrangements are all available from the UNC Jazz Press. Kirby Shaw's *Junior Jazz: Beginning Steps to Singing Jazz*, published by Hal Leonard, is also an excellent source for teaching beginning blues improvisation.

One effective assignment is to have the singers find a recorded blues improvisation by a favorite artist (vocal or instrumental) and memorize a twelve-bar chorus from it. Some student favorites include "Freddie Freeloader" by Jon Hendricks and Friends on A&M Records and "The E and D Blues" by Ella Fitzgerald from *The Duke Ellington Songbook* on Polydor. Students can study the excerpt by writing it out or by listening repeatedly. Give the assignment during the first week of class and tell students to be ready to sing it in class by midterm with a recorded blues accompaniment. Insert their twelve-bar solos into the blues arrangement that the choir is working on, which will usually involve changing the key of the original solo and securing the scale degree on which the solo begins. By concert time, all students should be able to sing a twelve-bar solo in the blues style.

Though it is true that the students will not be improvising at that point, they will be learning the improvisatory language of jazz by singing the masters' "licks" and by hearing the other singers' transcribed solos. After a year of improvisation rehearsals, students will have enough training to start developing a jazz language of their own and begin using quotations from other musicians' scats.

Finally, it is essential to examine the qualities of a "good" vocal improvisation. Certainly, its authenticity is judged by whether it swings and whether the scat syllables and the tonal language (scales/chord, licks, riffs, quotes, and so on) are appropriate. However, the solo will need more than authenticity to be an interesting solo.

Have students analyze what makes some solos more effective than others. An overall plan of motive, development, climax, and release gives a solo continuity. Some climactic devices include repetition, extremes in range, dramatic use of tone color, increased volume, ascending lines, dissonances, wide intervals, and double time. Some relaxation devices include decreased volume, descending lines, notes of longer duration, rests, legato, and consonance. By varying these elements, singers can produce dramatic effects that lend the element of surprise or unpredictability to their improvisations, which helps to keep them interesting.

It should be repeated that self-evaluation through tape-recordings is a useful tool when learning to improvise. Students can assess their own attempts at improvisation and decide what they would (perhaps) like to alter to make it more interesting, effective, or satisfying the next time.

It is possible for vocal students to learn jazz improvisation with integrity in the classroom. For more information on the sequential teaching of jazz to all ages and types of music classes, see the MENC publication, developed in conjunction with IAJE (International Association of Jazz Educators), *Teaching Jazz: A Course of Study* (1996). Teachers are encouraged to make every effort to provide their students with these techniques and opportunities to fully appreciate and participate in this unique American art form (Madura, 1997).

Chapter 6

Classical Choral Improvisation

Improvisation has long been a part of vocal music, and the National Standards for Music Education recommend that choral singers be able to improvise. However, there is little classical choral literature today that suggests improvisation. Most of the choral music that calls for improvisation is avant-garde in nature.

To address historical performance practice with regard to improvisation opportunities in choral music, choral directors must be creative. First, they must remember that in order to improvise in any style, the singer must have models to imitate. In order to teach Renaissance or Baroque style improvisation, the teacher must provide students with recorded and scored models, as well as enough working knowledge of the music theory needed to understand the style. This chapter will provide guidelines that will make adding authentic improvisation to your standard choral literature a new possibility.

Medieval

Extemporization was integral to early music performance. There is evidence that even Gregorian chants were ornamented and that many highly melismatic chants are actually notated versions of embellished simpler chants (Greenberg & Maynard, 1975). In vocal counterpoint of the fifteenth century, English Discant involved improvising upper parts over a notated chant melody, called a "cantus firmus" (Dart, 1963). There was a preference for parallel motion in thirds and sixths above the melody, as well as unisons with the cantus firmus at the beginning of the piece and at each cadence. With the fauxbourdon style of the Burgundian school and such composers as DuFay and Binchois, the cantus firmus was placed in the top or middle voice and it was improvised according the rules above, while the other parts were often notated (Ferand, 1961).

An outstanding resource for improvising to medieval chants in the rehearsal is Alice Parker's (1976) *Creative Hymn Singing*. She suggests teaching unison chant singing first, on such melodies as Benedictine plainsong and Praetorius's "Puer Nobis Nascitur." Then, some students may accompany the chant by singing pedal tones or ostinato at the tonic and the fifth. Later, parts may be added in organum, singing the melody at the fourth or fifth, or with three-part parallel motion in thirds and sixths, as described above. The choral director who teaches these different approaches to embellish a chant in medieval style enables students to develop their musical ear and exposes them to various methods of performance practice.

Renaissance

Training in improvisation, or "extemporaneous ornamentation" (Robinson & Winold, 1992, p. 355), was basic to the education of choral singers of the sixteenth century. Any vocal ensemble, professional or amateur, could improvise any genre of music. Often, they would decide on the particular places for and the types of ornamentation before each performance, or the lead singer of each voice part would perform the embellishments while the rest of the section sang the unadorned melody.

Diminution was a type of ornamentation that was common to almost all forms of secular and sacred music, including psalms, hymns, madrigals, and chanson but excluding the Ordinary of the Mass. Diminution refers to the breaking up of long melody notes into smaller note values in many different ways, including passing tones, melismas, and scale runs. This is usually done over expressive words. The top voice is the most suited to diminution; the bass voice is the least.

Freely improvised diminution occurred frequently in Renaissance music. No two singers improvised in exactly the same way, nor did a singer improvise the same piece in the same way twice (Greenberg & Maynard, 1975). Helpful manuals suggested formulas for ornamenting specific intervals as a way to avoid problems in ornamenting a line of a polyphonic work (Horsley, Collins, Badura-Skoda, & Libby, 1995). Examples can be found in a pamphlet titled *Choral Ornamentation* by Ray Robinson (1977). To help students learn to add ornaments spontaneously, they can be guided into writing out the ornaments, practicing them, and then incorporating them into other sixteenth century choral works.

Some basic guidelines during the Renaissance period suggested that ornamentation should be used in moderation; sound spontaneous; occur on long notes or important words; occur in only one part at a time, unless controlled by specified rules; and not occur at the beginning of a piece but should gradually increase as the piece progressed (Greenberg & Maynard, 1975.)

Alice Parker (1976) suggests that choral singers may take a Psalter hymn from the Renaissance, such as "Old Hundredth," and experiment with different voicings of its original four-part harmony. Each verse might be different, as in the following cases:

- everyone sings in unison, or just men sing or just women sing
- only the soprano and bass lines are sung, in either the high or low range
- alternatives are made, such as unison and SATB, or two equal SATB choirs, or choir and quartet

Parker also suggests exploring rhythmic possibilities with the text by alternating metric rhythm with free meter, giving important words or syllables two pulses.

Baroque

Melodic embellishment extended into practically every form of vocal music of the Baroque period. Emotional qualities in singing were emphasized, with dotted rhythms to communicate sighing, and spontaneous ornamentation began to be replaced by a trend toward stereotyped formulas for the trillo (an accelerated repetition of a single pitch), gruppo, tremolo, minuta, and more to be used over accented, emotion-filled words (Ferand, 1961). This trend is not unlike the dozens of melodic formulas that many contemporary jazz musicians learn to integrate into their improvisations.

Besides being written out with special signs or notation, these ornaments may also be produced where no indication exists. They can be added where there are musical similarities to passages where the ornaments do exist. Other examples of Baroque ornaments and their applications to actual choral pieces can be found in Robinson's (1977) monograph.

Parker (1976) suggests letting Bach's cantatas guide us in creating interesting and authentic improvisations by not beginning, but ending, with a four-part setting. For example in "Ein Feste Burg," start with the melody in the soprano and let the text determine when it might be appropriate to add another voice part, such as the bass. The director and the students, together, can decide on different combinations of parts. The melody can be traded between the sopranos and the tenors. Possible combinations include S, SB, SAB, SAT, TB, STB, SAT, and finally, SATB.

Classical

Vocal improvisation during the second half of the eighteenth century was controlled by two contradictory trends: virtuosity and classical simplicity. Free embellishment of melodies and cadenzas was the major type of vocal improvisation. Free improvisation during arias occurred on simple passages or on repetitions (Horsley et al., 1995). Improvisation also might have included a variety of the following devices: diminution, augmentation, appoggiaturas, trills, turns, staccato, legato, rubato, changing dynamics, and "everything else that enhances the effect of the voice" (Horsley et al., 1995, p. 45). Proper declamation of the text and expression were of foremost importance, and minimal ornamentation of "i" and "u" vowels was suggested. The application of the ornaments to secondary-level choral music can be found in Robinson's (1977) *Choral Ornamentation,* and suggestions for adding variety through changing voicings and dynamics can be found in Parker's (1976) *Creative Hymn Singing.*

In the music of Mozart, Haydn, and Beethoven, most of the ornamentations were notated, and improvisatory freedom became increasingly restricted. Singers were obliged to perform the following embellishments, even when not notated: appoggiaturas, embellishment of the fermatas at cadential points, and final cadenzas of concertos, where often an elaboration of the themes of the concerto was sung at the fermata. Skilled improvisation was clearly no longer expected of the average musician.

Romantic

Improvisation skill began to die out in the nineteenth century. Ornaments, such as diminutions and cadenzas, were usually written out in a defense against the trend toward superficial, unmusical, and unexpressive improvisations that were being performed for the sake of virtuosity only. Also, an increase in amateur musicians who had little knowledge of ornamentation furthered the necessity of having ornaments notated (Horsley et al., 1995).

Improvised vocal cadenzas survived the first half of the nineteenth century. They consisted of embellishments of the dominant chord near the end of the piece. They were sung in one breath, began with a messa di voce, and ended with a trill on the supertonic, with added ornamentation if desired (Horsley et al., 1995). While virtuoso vocal solo parts were often ornamented in the nineteenth century, choral parts were not. Therefore, we will proceed to the twentieth century, when choral improvisation was brought back to life.

Twentieth Century

Spirituals

Most school choral ensembles perform spirituals, but few include improvisation in their performances. Start with a familiar, slow song such as "Sometimes I Feel like a Motherless Child," or an up-tempo "Standin' in the Need of Prayer," and let everyone improvise. Songs from the *Sister Act II Songbook* also work well, such as "Ain't No Mountain," "Pay Attention," and "His Eye Is on the Sparrow." Start by getting everyone to feel the beat together. Begin to let students play with the text, rhythms, or phrase structure. Let them sing other melodies simultaneously or talk back and forth to the main melody. Don't criticize. The only thing that may not be altered is the beat. Communication is the most important thing (Parker, 1976). Even the most sophisticated of musicians who are used to reading the score will enjoy the sense of freedom and play that this experience holds. Later, the techniques used in improvising to a simple melody may be added to choral scores of spirituals, such as "Joyful, Joyful," arranged by Warren and adapted by Emerson for SATB, SSA, and two-part choir, and "Ezekiel Saw de Wheel" by Dawson for a mixed chorus of up to twelve parts.

A good vehicle for this type of improvisation is the two-part arrangement of the spiritual "Chatter with the Angels" by Charles Collins, published by Boosey & Hawkes. Section III is perfect for spontaneous harmonization and responses, as it is written in unison and arranged in the gospel format of repetition (in this case, of a minor third) with gradual accelerando. This piece also offers an improvisation section between sections I and II, where the pentatonic scale is encouraged. Improvised, chattering angel voices also may be added.

Modal

For a modal improvisation experience, try "Blues à la Mode" by David Ward-Steinman (see figure 1). It is intended for SATB, with an improvised solo and optional rhythm section. The piece uses the familiar twelve-bar blues format described in previous chapters, but in place of the traditional primary chords used in the blues, this piece imaginatively substitutes the Phrygian mode for the I chord, the Lydian mode for the IV chord, and the Dorian mode for the V chord. The rhythm section (piano, bass, and drums) may function as in a typical jazz format (swinging, walking bass line, off-beat piano 'comping). Although the format is jazz-like, the chord progression and modal language are not; thus, this piece can provide a bridge between jazz and other types of modal improvisation.

Aleatory

"Aleatory," "chance music," and "indeterminacy" are terms that refer to works composed since 1945 that involve leaving some elements of the musical structure open to the performer's choice (Apel, 1977). It is interesting to note that almost all of the choral literature that provides improvisation opportunities is aleatoric. Some pieces are mainly traditional choral works with short sections of aleatory, while others are completely aleatoric. Some provide freedom with speaking words and unusual sounds, while others specify freedom with particular pitches and rhythms. Some are written in traditional notation and others use graphic notation. Several pieces appropriate for K–12 choirs are recommended in this chapter.

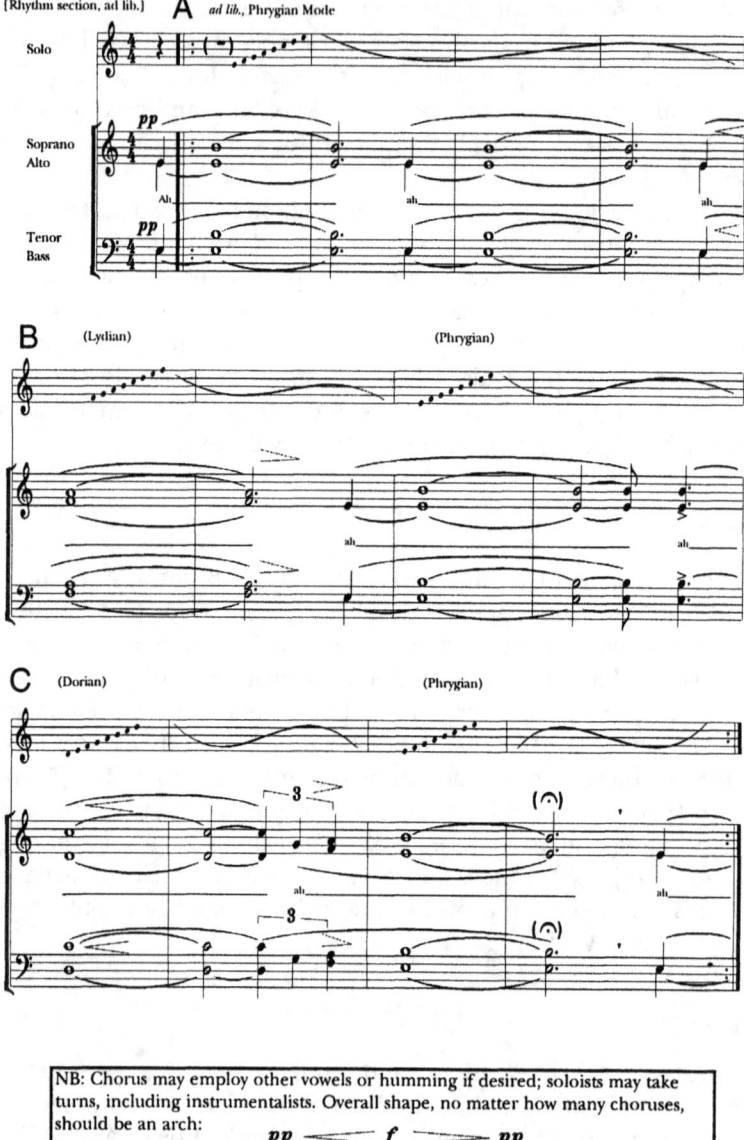

Figure 1. A composition that can be used for modal improvisation.

Traditional Notation with Short Sections of Aleatoric Sound Effects. A good example for teaching beginning improvised sound effects is Goetze's *Sing as the Prairie* for two-part treble voices, published by Boosey & Hawkes. It includes short sections of wind sounds made with "sh" or "ss" sounds or whistles, interspersed with traditional tonal harmony. At the climax, to symbolize being overcome by the "merciless grasp of the blizzard," the voices divide up to sustain the accented "s" sounds. During the next four measures, children use vocal sounds to indicate the building intensity of the blizzard and its eventual subsiding, ending with sounds of the prairie after the storm.

Traditional Notation with Short Sections of Aleatoric Rhythm. Rupert Lang's "Cantate Domino" for SSA divisi, published by Boosey & Hawkes, includes two short measures of indeterminacy, where each voice sings the text in any rhythm and enters at any time. A unison pitch for each voice part is specified for all words. The two texts that are sung freely are "Laus eius in ecclesia sanctorum" ("Praise Him in His Holy Church") and "Exultent in rege suo" ("They rejoice in their King"), perhaps suggesting that each person praises in his or her own way. The rest of the piece is tonal, accompanied by synthesizer, and of medium difficulty.

"Exultet Coelum Laudibus" by John Paynter, published by Oxford University Press, is a similar example of indeterminacy in that each singer improvises freely with the note groups for that voice part, giving the effect of "one of many voices together but independent." The order of the pitches may not be changed, but rhythm and tempos are free. In this SATB divisi composition, the opening measure is improvised on the word "Alleluya," and the final three measures are improvised on the words, "Then be all merry in this house, Exultet." Paynter emphasizes the importance of keeping the passages from becoming rigid in any way by avoiding mechanical repetition. Soprano and tenor solos are also free with regard to tempo.

James Grant's "Psalm 98," published by Earthsongs, includes seven measures of indeterminacy out of 115 measures of SATB divisi. At letter E, each of the eight parts is freely chanted on unison pitches of E, F#, G#, A#, C#, D#, E, and F# "with no synchronization within sections; the entrances of each section, however, should be very regular, as notated." Entrances are staggered with the following text: "Let the sea make a noise" (three voice parts); "the sea and all that is in it" (two parts); "the sea and the lands" (one part); and "the lands and all those who dwell therein" (two parts). Letter F continues with no synchronization within each voice part, but with regular entrances, and each singer sings the following rhythm at an independent tempo:

The text is "Let the rivers clap their hands," in all but the S2 part, which sings, "Let the rivers clap! clap! clap! clap!" with an altered rhythm. The unison pitches for each voice part are (starting from B2): G, A, B, C#, D, E; and F# for S1 and S2.

Traditional Notation with Aleatoric Phrases. "The Swallow" for SSAA by Nancy Telfer, published by Kjos, introduces the concept of aleatoric music with helpful instructions to the singers and effective teaching strategies for directors. At three separate measures, each singer chooses between two different melodic themes but starts at a different time and tempo from the next singer and repeats that theme until the conductor's downbeat for the next measure. In each case, the improvised measure lasts for ten seconds. In the last five measures, the text "Swallow, go higher, fly" is written in an ascending line, in four-part canon, to create the image of the swallows rising in the sky. Each singer is again free to improvise the tempo, while the conductor varies the length of each measure and the dynamics.

René Clausen's "All That Hath Life and Breath" for SATB divisi choir includes a short section of indeterminacy for the sopranos, who enter one at a time and may sing any or all of three melodic themes in the key of G major. The three texts are "All that have life and breath praise ye the Lord," "Praise the Lord with joyful song," and "Alleluia!"

Graphic Notation

Graphic notation "gives no precise indication of what notes are to be played, or when, but uses graphic means...to suggest what the performer might play" (Sadie, 1988). "Here Comes the Avant-Garde" by Brock McElheran is an enjoyable choral piece meant to familiarize choirs and audiences with many twentieth century compositional techniques. Any combination of at least ten singers is needed, as well as a narrator and pianist. The score is presented in three columns, one with the narrator's words, the second with the graphic notation for the singers, and the third with directions for the singers. The singers make their own interpretation of the following vocal sounds: tinkles, rumbles, laughter, shouts, gasps, whistles, tongue clicks, quarter tones, blots, plops, specks, tickas, arrows, oops, unvoiced explosive consonants, glissandos, and ten different pitches that are interpretations of different shapes (rectangles, triangles, and diamonds). The piece is moderately easy and is available from Oxford University Press.

An entire series called "Music for Young Players" is published by Universal Edition and features graphic scores for performance by any music class, and some pieces are appropriate for choral ensembles. No knowledge of traditional notation is needed. The following compositions are suitable for choirs wishing to explore graphic scores: "Autumn" for voices and instruments by John Paynter, "Sound Patterns

I" and "Sound Patterns III" by Bernard Rands, "Miniwanka" and "Minimusic" by Murray Schafer, and "Take a Shape" by George Self.

Paynter's "Autumn" is in unison and easy, thus making it a good introduction to graphic notation as a "sound picture." It is intended for ten- and twelve-year-olds who can sing in the range of middle C to one octave higher and suggests glockenspiel and metallophone accompaniment, although other instruments will work. The mood is the sadness of autumn and is set up by random raindrop sounds from the instruments. The sung melody consists of whole notes and fermatas on the text "The falling leaves fall and pile up. The rain beats on the rain." Singers choose their own tempos and durations, but all start together in unison. At the fermatas, all singers sustain their pitches until everyone arrives. The conductor gives signals to indicate when to move on to the next measure, at least six seconds from the beginning of the measure.

"Sound Patterns I" by Rands is scored for voices and hands. The choir is divided into four groups. The voice notation includes graphic symbols for voiced sounds, both staccato and sustained, and varying pitches; for unvoiced sounds, both sustained and varied; and for tongue clicks. Symbols for the hands indicate a single clap, fast sustained clapping, fingers snapping, hands rubbing together, and mouth patting. The score also includes some text, dynamic markings, and one staff line per part to indicate the middle register of the voice. Symbols above and below that line indicate approximate pitches. Measures are approximately five seconds apart and downbeats are given by the conductor. At all times, singers are encouraged to experiment and listen.

"Sound Patterns III" by Rands uses similar symbols to those in "Sound Patterns I," but the goal is to explore the sound possibilities of speech. Individuals should bring any paragraph of text to the rehearsal, and all should read aloud simultaneously. Then the class can alter their normal manner of reading by exploring duration, tempo, articulation, volume, and register. Other possibilities for exploration include speaking only monosyllables or consonants, or using the hands to muffle sounds. The spatial dimension can be explored by arranging students in different parts of the room. The goal is to help singers develop imaginative approaches to improvisation. For performance, the number of texts could be limited to four.

In "Minimusic" by Murray Schafer, each page of score is divided into three parts by dotted lines from left to right, which are to be cut so that the singer can turn any third of the page either forward or backward. These "boxes" are numbered from 1 to 36. Each box has arrows indicating which direction the singers may proceed, forward or back a page and up or down a box. All singers begin in Box 1 but not simultaneously. Any number of pages may be turned, but having arrived at a box, the singer must sing it. Numbers in each box refer to the duration in seconds. Boxes contain graphic notation and/or written directions. Here are a few of the boxes' written directions: "Sing +2 (major second) below the loudest sound you hear," "Do exactly opposite of what the singer on your right is doing," "Sing two lines of a hymn or a hymn-like tune," and "Wait for a pause in the sound, then produce one emphatic effect in an unorthodox way." The piece ends when all of the performers stop singing; then they turn to the final page and perform it in unison. Since "Minimusic" is an exercise in improvisation and ear training, each performer must listen and be able to hear each of the other performers.

"Epitaph for Moonlight" is probably Schafer's most-performed choral work. Although written for youth choir (SATB divisi) and optional bells, it is often performed by high school, university, and professional choral ensembles. The text was created by seventh graders and includes sound synonyms for the students' concepts of moonlight. They include: "Nu-yu-yul," "Maunklinde," "Malooma," "Lunious," "Shiverglowa," "Shalowa," and "Neshmoor." Like "Minimusic," this piece is an ear-training exercise in that "singers must learn to pitch their notes by interval from any note given." The piece begins with S1 humming "a medium high note ad lib.," followed by S2 entering a whole step lower, S3 another whole step lower, S4 another whole step lower, and so on through B4. This creates a two-and-a-half octave whole tone scale occurring over twenty seconds in time. The score is entirely in graphic notation, with dynamics indicated by thickness of line. Also included are a circle of improvised pitches and rhythms by the soprano and altos; wavy lines for individual parts to improvise, first with neighbor tones and then more freely; blank ovals where particular voice parts are silent; glissandos; and whispers. This is a fine piece for introducing your choir to graphic notation and aleatoric improvisation, while improving aural skills. It is an effective performance piece, as well.

Other recommended Schafer pieces that include unusual uses of the voice, graphic notation, and indeterminacy are "Snowforms" for SA, published by Arcana Editions; "The Star Princess and the Waterlilies," for SA with soloists, narrator, Orff instruments, and percussion, published by Arcana Editions; and "A Garden of Bells," for SATB divisi, published by Arcana Editions. "Hear Me Out," for four voices, uses mostly spoken text of well-known figures of speech, like the following:

- "Keep your ear to the ground"
- "Put your money where your mouth is"
- "Ring up a sale"

- "Money talks"
- "In a manner of speaking"
- "That rings a bell"
- "Sound off"
- "You can buy it for a song"
- "All you have to do is whistle"
- "The call of the wild"
- "Silence is golden"
- "Sounds good to me."

Pauline Oliveros's chance compositions have withstood the test of time, and every student should experience an Oliveros composition and its meditative and liberating effects at least once. A few of her many interesting improvisatory works for voices include "Oh Ha Ha," "Sonic Meditations," and "Meditation on the Points of a Compass," all published by Earthsongs.

Dedicated to Oliveros is Ron Jeffers's "Sanctus," also published by Earthsongs. In "Sanctus," each voice expresses whatever it considers to be "holy." A Japanese bowl gong (or large handbell or tubular chime) begins the piece with three very long tones. "Sometime" after the second gong has sounded, the altos sing three given pitches on the word "Sanctus," with free duration but within one long breath. They repeat freely. Later, the bowl gong sounds another three long tones. "Sometime" after the first of those three gongs, the tenors do the same as the altos, but with different pitches. The sopranos begin after the next pattern of three long gong tones; and then the gong sounds twice. After the first, the basses intone their phrase; and "sometime" after the second, the altos sing a new phrase three times. Then the tenors sing their new phrase three times, followed by the sopranos and the basses. "Sometime" during this section of the piece, the gong sounds one final time. Then each singer returns to his or her original phrase, and the altos fade out first, followed by the tenors, sopranos, and basses.

An outstanding and very accessible resource for avant-garde vocal performances is *Scores: An Anthology of New Music* (1981) selected by Roger Johnson and published by Schirmer. Chapters for vocalists include "Exercises, Rituals, and Meditations" (including Oliveros's "Sonic Meditations"); "Music for Voices," which includes speech-sound pieces; choral and ensemble music; and solo voice music. The other chapters for instruments, electronic music, and theater are equally interesting.

Chapter 7
World Music Improvisation

Improvisation is central to much of the world's music. Choral music provides one avenue for world music improvisation to be introduced into the classroom. Two ways that world music improvisation can be approached are discussed in the following examples. Some pieces use avant-garde musical language while employing references to and texts of other cultures, like the examples discussed under *Canada* and *Sweden*. However, these pieces often make no attempt to use the authentic musical language of that culture. Others, such as those published by World Music Press, feature authentic melodies and texts from other cultures, but they give little specific guidance with regard to improvisation. The remainder of the chapter are examples of this method of improvisation. (See the World Music Improvisation Discography sidebar for artists and selections that can be used to teach this chapter in the classroom.)

Vocal improvisation has a long history in both the traditional and the art music of many cultures. Traditional music, also known as folk music, tends to be relatively simple, compared to sophisticated classical music styles. Both traditional and art music are introduced here, along with musical suggestions for the classroom, in hopes of generating greater interest in world music improvisation.

Canada

"Keewaydin," is an example of the first category: It uses references to other cultures and some of their texts, but it does not use the authentic musical language of those cultures. This SSA selection includes an optional tape by Harry Freedman, whose text is derived from the language of the Ojibwa Indian nation and is made up of names of places found in Ontario. It uses a graphic score and stresses interval relationships, particularly major and minor seconds and thirds from any sounding pitch. At one point, each singer may choose from twelve different phrases to sing in any order. Later, they excitedly speak any combination of another twelve phrases.

Sweden

Also in the first category, and composed for SSA, is "Aglepta" by Arne Mellnas, published by Walton. This is a moderately difficult avant-garde and aleatoric piece commissioned by the Swedish Broadcasting Company in Stockholm. The piece uses the following nineteenth century invocation from the Swedish region of Smaland: "Aglaria Pidhol aria Ananus Qepta." The troll proverb translates as, "To leave an enemy without an answer, say these words to him and blow in his direction." Aleatoric sections involve each singer in improvising pitches and durations, as well as singing the highest or lowest pitch possible.

Brazil

In the second category is "Tres Cantos Nativos dos Indios Krao" by Marcos Leite. Published by Earthsongs, this piece is described as "freely based on melodies sung by the Krao tribe—a group of native Brazilian Indians who live in the Singu river area of the Amazonia forest of northwestern Brazil." Although this SATB piece is in traditional notation, improvisation occurs twice: at the beginning of the first canto and the end of the second canto, where sopranos and altos improvise animal cries, as well as rain, river, and wind sounds to imitate the atmosphere of the rain forest jungle. The text is in Spanish phonemes and includes a pronunciation guide.

Africa

For other examples of authenticity in multicultural choral music, look to World Music Press. From South Africa, "Somagwaza" is arranged by Pete Seeger for SATB. It is a ceremonial song that is used in the initiation of the young men of a community into adult status. It is suggested by the publisher that this arrangement is not the only interpretation of the ancient song and that the notation is inadequate to "convey the intricacies of rhythm and suspended syncopation." Freedom of expression is strongly encouraged, but no specific improvisation is suggested. However, it is important to note that in many African music selections, there are no real differences between memorized songs and improvisatory variations on them. It is typical to vary musical themes or motives in every performance (Nettl, Capwell, Bohlman, Wong, & Turino, 1992).

"Chi Chi Cha!" is based on the marimba band styles of the Shona people of Zimbabwe, written by Judith Cook Tucker for SATB, piano, and percussion. At the end of this driving, polyrhythmic work, Cook suggests improvising by repeating any and all vocal parts together to reach a climax and then reversing the order of the sections, working backwards from section H to section B and ending with the opening piano vamp.

"Vamudara," a traditional dance song from Zimbabwe, is arranged for SATB and percussion by Dumisana Maraire. It is in 12/8 time (2+2+2+3+3) and written in the Shona language. As in "Somagwaza," his arrangement is not necessarily the definitive version of this piece.

In Zimbabwe, this song might be sung this particular way only once. The score notes say to "improvise freely."

North America

The music of Native Americans and Southern Appalachian communities can provide improvisatory opportunities for classroom activity. African-American music is not included here as it has already been described in chapters 4, 5, and 6 under the categories of Gospel, Blues, Jazz, and Spirituals. (While African-American music is certainly a world music, with its mixture of African and European musical elements, it is such a complex part of American musical culture that it requires its own chapters.)

Native Americans

The voice is the primary means of expression in the traditional music of Native Americans, and it is often accompanied by drums, rattles, and dance in duple meter. Phrases often begin on high pitches and descend. Syllables such as "weeya," "heya," "weehee," "ho," "ne," and "yo" are used frequently. In the classroom, children may use these native syllables and improvise tetratonic (four-note) or pentatonic (five-note) melodies; or they may create nature poems in duple meter and improvise pentatonic melodies to accompany them. They may add rhythm patterns with drums and ceremonial dances, while improvising animal sounds and nature sounds. Repetition should be plentiful (Anderson & Campbell, 1996). Native American songs that can be used as models for vocal improvisation can be found in Hackett's (1998) *The Melody Book*.

Southern Appalachia

The music of the Southern Appalachian mountains originates from the seventeenth century immigrants from the British Isles and was passed orally from generation to generation. These vocal ballads, songs, and games can be found in many children's songbooks. As with any folk music, a long oral tradition results in many variants (often hundreds) of a melody, which explains why we see and hear so many versions of a single folk song in textbooks and recordings. There is usually no "correct" version. Thus, the expression and interpretation of a tune are left to the discretion of the individual singer (Anderson and Campbell, 1996). Students should listen to various recordings of the same song for interpretive ideas related to text, dynamics, tempo, rhythm, phrasing, singing style, articulation, and accompaniment.

> **World Music Improvisation**
>
> Bennett, Geetha. *Veena.* Cassette, 1995. Sangeetha 6 ECDB 493.
> Bennett, Geetha Ramanathan. *Carnatic Heritage.* CD, 1993. Sangita G&FB 1993.
> *The Best of World Music, Volume 1: World Vocal.* Cassette, 1993. Rhino R4 71203.
> *Celtic Aura: The Irish Traditional Music Special.* CD, 1998. Gael-Linn CDTCD-X 008.
> *Celtic Mouth Music.* CD and Book, 1997. Ellipsis Arts 4070.
> *Global Voices.* 3 CDs, 1998. Music of the World 146, 147, 148.
> *Indonesia–Madura: Art Music.* CD, 1995. Ocora C 560083.
> *Iran: Persian Classical Music.* CD, 1991. Elektra Nonesuch Explorer 9 72060-2.
> *Ireland's Greatest Hits.* CD, 1996. RCA 07863 66813-2.
> *Making Connections: Multicultural Music and the National Standards.* CD, 1998. MENC 3000.
> Ramanathan, S. *Tyagaraja's Songs on Music, Volume 1.* Cassette, 1988. Veena 001.
> *Royal Court Music of Thailand.* CD. Smithsonian Folkways 40413.
> *Thailand: Ka Samui.* CD, 1998. Sunset France SA 141023.
> *Traditional Music: The Cycle of Life.* Cassette, 1997. Yayasan Daya Putih Foundation Bali 1997.

Europe

Traditional music styles of Europe differ from culture to culture, although certain musical traditions of Europe seem to be universal. Strophic form is common with verses and refrains. Most music is metric with recurring accents. Duple and triple meters are the most common, but the irregular meters of 5/8 and 7/8 can also be found (Anderson & Campbell, 1996).

Ireland

Irish traditional music relies on ornamentation for its interest more than anything else. Unison duet singing is common, with variations on the melody sung simultaneously. Accompaniment is rare, but if it exists, it is very simple. Melodies and their embellishments are based on pentatonic, Ionian, Aeolian, Dorian, and Mixolydian modes.

While the bulk of Irish traditional music is fast and in duple or triple meter, it is the slower Irish airs, especially those with a wide vocal range, that are conducive to extensive embellishment. These ornamented airs, however, are not held to regular meter. The Irish verse, which may contain irregularly metered, unstressed syllables, determines both the rhythm of the ornaments and the tempo of the song (Bodley & Breathnach, 1995).

A unique form of ornamentation that is characteristic of Irish singing is a rhythmic device of stopping the breath. The first note of a melodic line might be split in this way, or a final unaccented note might be accented and short. Another device is the ornamentation of the main melodic note with grace notes, turns, passing tones, and glissando (Bodley & Breathnach, 1995).

Singers also occasionally add spoken comments, such as "said he" and "she says," or speak the final word or phrase of a song. As is common in much folk singing, a slightly nasal vocal quality is often used, but vibrato, great dynamic variety, and other dramatic devices are unusual.

Teachers can look for various recordings of Irish airs, such as the favorite and familiar "Danny Boy," and have the class compare different versions of the same song. They can try to reduce it to a basic melody by identifying any embellishments and then try to sing it plain. After practicing the various ways of ornamenting an Irish air, based on recorded examples and the suggestions given above, students may try embellishing other Irish airs on their own.

Mediterranean Europe

It should be mentioned that Spain, Italy, and Greece have contributed highly ornamented melodies to the world's folk music. Other unique characteristics of Mediterranean singing include a slightly nasal tone quality, heterophony (simultaneous variations on the melodies), and the use of minor melodies and augmented seconds (Anderson & Campbell, 1996).

Eastern Europe

The traditional music of Poland, the Czech Republic, Hungary, Romania, Bulgaria, and Yugoslavia also use frequent melodic ornamentation, heterophony, and irregular or free meter (Anderson & Campbell, 1996).

"Zol Zain Sholem" ("Let There Be Peace") is a Yiddish Song from Eastern Europe. It is written for SATB, soloist, and piano accompaniment, and is very accessible. On the repetitions of the song, different voices may sing the verses and refrains. They may alternate among soloist, females, males, high voices, low voices, and so on. These evaluative decisions can be made jointly by the singers and the director.

Classical Music of Asia and the Middle East

"In the classical music of India and the Middle East, improvised and composed music coexist...as distinct processes" (Nettl et al., 1992, p. 62-63). It is important to realize, however, that improvisation without advance preparation is unthinkable in Asian and Middle Eastern music. A musician spends many years memorizing traditional composed models and listening to masters' improvisations before attempting any original improvisation.

South Asia

Improvisation is essential to the art music of India. It occurs in the melodic line while being accompanied by a drone and percussion. The soloist may also be accompanied in unison by other instruments, creating heterophony. The major constraint in south Asian music is the Indian modal form, the raga. Students are required to "memorize lengthy compositions in each raga so that the features of the ragas embodied in them will be absorbed" (Jairazbhoy, 1995, p. 53).

While most Western musicians are more familiar with the music of the North Indian classical tradition (Hindustani culture), vocal music is more important in South India, where instrumentalists play vocal tunes and imitate vocal articulations. The musical forms are similar in the two traditions, but use different terms. In the South Indian tradition, singers often perform etudes (kritis) with an improvised introduction in a particular mode (ragam). The first section (alapanam) has no regular pulse, but the ragam is explored with increasingly extensive use of range and proceeds into the next section (tanam), which has a pulse but no meter. After this improvised introduction, the metered kritis often contain one of two types of improvisation. In the first type (niraval), the text is maintained while the pitches of the ragam are used to improvise a new melody. In the second (svarakalpana), the names of the pitches are sung instead of the text, as in solfège singing. In listening, the way to determine when improvisation occurs is when the accompaniment, often a violin, is no longer playing in unison with the singer (Nettl et al., 1992). Indian improvisation lessons appropriate for the classroom, including explanations of the various Indian ragas, can be found in Anderson and Campbell's (1996) *Multicultural Perspectives in Music Education*.

Middle East

Middle Eastern music is similar to Indian music in three ways: (1) modal forms (Turkish maqam and Persian dastgah) are the basis for highly ornamented improvisation; (2) the music is divided into two sections: an unmeasured section (Arabic taqsim and Persian avaz) and the metric sections (tasnif, reng, beste, and bashraf), which are often accompanied by drums; and (3) the music often has a rich heterophonic texture, where ornamentation, whether melodic, rhythmic, or timbral, embellishes and supports the melody (Jairazbhoy, 1995).

The avaz is Persian classical poetry that is sung. Although the avaz is nonmetric, the long and short syllables of the verse determine the rhythm of the modal improvisation (Jairazbhoy, 1995). The development of the avaz is based on gradual expansion of the vocal range and is where most of the improvisation occurs. Ornaments include added notes, removal of notes, turns, tremolos, and drones. Lesson plans for familiarizing students with Middle Eastern music and its modes may be found in Anderson and Campbell's (1996) *Multicultural Perspectives in Music Education.*

East and Southeast Asia

Some improvisation occurs in east Asia (China, Japan, and Korea) and southeast Asia (Indonesia, Thailand, Laos, Vietnam, and Burma), but when it does, it is usually instrumental. However, even in the instrumental gamelan music of the Indonesian islands of Java and Madura, it is the dalang, the master reciter and singer of the great epic cycles, who is also a virtuosic vocal improviser. These great dramas (the Madurese Mahabharata and the Javanese Ramayana), which include actors, dancers, instrumentalists, and puppets, are controlled by the dalang who directs the show with his voice and small iron clappers in his hands. These signal the important entries and structural points of the epic drama, which often lasts all night long. The dalang's knowledge of the legends and the psychology of their characters is so deep that he improvises freely during the drama, using timbre and diction very expressively. While the music of Madura uses the slendro scale exclusively (pentatonic), Java uses both the slendro and the pelog (heptatonic) scales (Jakar, 1995). Indonesian gamelan music is fascinating to study, and fortunately, there are many opportunities to learn about it. In fact, there are approximately 200 gamelans located in the United States (Brown, 1997).

Vocal improvisation can be experienced in a lesson in classical Thai music. For an example, students can listen to any recording of Thai music from World Music Library or Smithsonian/Folkways. Two main characteristics of Thai music are the extensive use of pentatonic melodies and heterophonic texture in which many layers of the same melody occur simultaneously. Melodic embellishment is integral to an interesting performance. Since the melodies are limited to pentatonic tones, singers can improvise pentatonic and rhythmic embellishment on any southeast Asian pentatonic tunes. The singers should converge on the written pitch every four measures as a structural reference point. Western instruments can be added, with xylophones, recorders, and metallophones playing or improvising to the original melody, while finger cymbals play on every beat, first ringing and then muted. One drum may play a simple ostinato, while another will play one stroke every two measures (Anderson & Campbell, 1996).

Summary

Improvisation in world music, as well as improvisation in any style, is learned in three primary ways: (1) by listening extensively to a particular culture's musical improvisations; (2) by vocally imitating recordings of that culture's improvisations; and (3) by studying the basic theoretical tools of that culture's music (e.g., scales, modes, rhythms, types of ornaments, meters, tempos, etc.).

Teachers can begin to familiarize themselves with world music improvisation in many ways, including:
- ordering recordings of world music from the *Music of the World* catalog (Phone: 919-932-9600) or your favorite comprehensive record store;
- taking world music classes that are offered at most universities and summer workshops, such as those sponsored by the College Music Society and the International Society for Music Education (ISME);
- inviting ethnic musicians in the community, often through cultural centers, to perform for classes; and
- consulting Anderson and Campbell's (1996) *Multicultural Perspectives in Music Education,* an outstanding resource for anyone interested in teaching about world music.

Chapter 8

Can and Should We Assess Vocal Improvisation?

Prerequisites

The National Standards for Music Education state that all students in grades K–12 should be able to improvise in very specific ways. However, before we can expect students to achieve the improvisation standards, they must be allowed and encouraged to express themselves creatively in music. Therefore, a balance must be achieved between allowing freedom of expression, without fear of being wrong, and expecting a particular level of improvisation competence. Here are several ways a teacher can work toward achieving this balance.

Students must be guided into vocal improvisation experiences that allow opportunities to explore the sound environment in a supportive, playful, and tension-free classroom or rehearsal. Fear is the enemy of the creative impulse.

Teachers should create enough structure in the lessons so that students know the boundaries of their improvisational freedom. Too much freedom is overwhelming. Have students improvise with musical materials with which they are already very familiar. This will give them the opportunity to choose from known possibilities.

Students need to feel that success is attainable. So at the beginning, limit improvisation choices to one thing at a time (changing the rhythm, pitches, words, dynamics, timbre, or range), only gradually increasing the challenge.

When students feel safe, know the rules of the game, and sense that they can succeed, they will relish the opportunity to express their individuality through vocal improvisation.

The Complete Musician

Wouldn't it be rewarding if young vocalists were able to read, notate, transcribe, perform, improvise, compose, and arrange with equal competency? In an ideal world, a student would be able to perform a recital piece and, in the event of a memory lapse, know the harmony, form, and performance practice well enough to be able to improvise competently and confidently until reaching a securely memorized place in the music. The improviser should become so informed about a particular style's or culture's musical practice that the improvisation will sound almost as musically sophisticated as a notated composition, yet retain the freshness and spontaneity that improvisation implies. To accomplish this, the teacher must view teaching improvisation as an important tool in creating the complete musician. There are historical precedents and national standards to support this premise. This book has attempted to present teaching strategies directed toward that goal.

VOCAL JAZZ IMPROVISATION MEASURE (VJIM)

Please rate each aspect of vocal jazz improvisation based on the following criteria:

1=Poor   2=Weak   3=Fair   4=Good   5=Excellent

1. Sense of pulse   1 2 3 4 5

2. Appropriate rhythmic feel (swing, Latin)   1 2 3 4 5

3. Appropriate jazz rhythmic figures   1 2 3 4 5
    (primarily eighth notes, syncopation)

4. Appropriate jazz language   1 2 3 4 5
    (riffs, licks, quotes, patterns, etc.)

5. Appropriate scat syllables   1 2 3 4 5

6. Correct note choices for harmonies   1 2 3 4 5

7. Intonation   1 2 3 4 5

8. Vocal quality and technique   1 2 3 4 5

9. Variety in vocal range   1 2 3 4 5

10. Variety in dynamics   1 2 3 4 5

11. Originality of musical ideas   1 2 3 4 5

12. Development and unity of ideas   1 2 3 4 5

Figure 1. A form for assessing jazz improvisation.

Assessment Strategies

But can we assess improvisation skills? Should we? We can and should. Assessment strategies are simple. Rating scales can be used easily, objectively, and effectively. The Vocal Jazz Improvisation Measure (VJIM) (Madura, 1995) is shown in Figure 1 and can be used to assess jazz improvisation, or it may be adapted by changing the criteria to fit free improvisation, structured improvisation, gospel ornamentation, classical extemporization, aleatoric improvisation, or world music improvisation. Design class objectives that specify the level of improvisation competency that is to be taught on a particular day. Start with the achievement standards of the National Standards for Music Education (as discussed in Chapter 1 of this book). It may be better not to use the general content standard 3: "Improvising melodies, variations, and accompaniments." Since the content standards are not written for specific grade levels, it is better to look to the specific achievement standards for objectives, such as that for grade 4, "Improvise simple rhythmic and melodic ostinato accompaniments," or for grade 8, "Improvise melodic embellishments and simple rhythmic and melodic variations on given pentatonic melodies and melodies in major keys."

Then, be sure to assess each individual's achievement of that objective. This can be accomplished by having students demonstrate their competence individually or in small groups, where you can see and hear each student's contribution. Beware of group activities where students are not assessed individually, because there are always a few gifted students who will make it sound as if the majority of the class is progressing. Listening to small groups of individuals takes more time, of course, but it ensures accurate assessment. Also, tape record the improvisations and keep them in a portfolio to measure individual musical growth several times throughout the school year.

Be sure students achieve all of the improvisation achievement standards for their particular grade level. They have at least four years (grades K–4, 5–8, and 9–12) to accomplish each set of achievement standards, so this should not be a problem. Combining the achievement standards of the National Standards for Music Education with the standards in *Opportunity-to-Learn Standards for Music Instruction: Grades PreK–12* (MENC, 1994) will make it simple for students to accomplish all of the improvisation achievement standards before high school graduation. It will be interesting to observe whether a generation of students who learn to improvise continues to participate in music activities as adults, as we hope they will.

References

Aebersold, J. (1988). *Nothin' but blues.* New Albany, IN: Aebersold.

Anderson, W. M., & Campbell P. S. (Eds.) (1996). *Multicultural perspectives in music education.* 2nd ed. Reston, VA: MENC.

Apel, W. (1977). *Harvard dictionary of music* (2nd ed.). Cambridge: Belknap.

Azzara, C. D., Grunow, R. F., & Gordon, E. E. (1997). *Creativity in improvisation.* Chicago: GIA.

Baker, B. W. (1983). "Gospel music: Popular alternatives for the urban schools." In C. E. Hicks, J. A. Standifer, & W. L. Carter (Eds.), *Methods and perspectives in urban music education.* Washington DC: University Press of America, 303–24, 470–83.

Baker, D. N. (1986). *How to play bebop 1, 2, & 3.* New York: Alfred.

Baker, D. N. (1988). *Jazz improvisation: A comprehensive method for all musicians* (rev. ed.). New York: Alfred.

Berg, S. (1998, April). "Teaching beginning improvisation in the jazz ensemble rehearsal." Paper presented at MENC's National Biennial In-Service Conference, Phoenix, AZ.

Bitz, M. (1998). "Teaching improvisation outside of jazz settings." *Music Educators Journal, 84* (4), 21–24, 41.

Bodley, S., & Breathnach, B. (1995). "Ireland." In S. Sadie (Ed.), *The new Grove dictionary of music and musicians* (Vol. 9). London: Macmillan.

Brown, R. E. (1997). [Interview with Director of Center for World Music, Payangan, Bali].

Cherry-blossoms: Japanese haiku series III (1969). New York: The Peter Pauper Press.

Choksy, L. (1988). *The Kodály method.* Englewood Cliffs, NJ: Prentice Hall.

Cox, D. (1995, February). "Vocal improvisation in gospel music." Paper presented at a meeting of the Ohio Music Education Association, Columbus.

Dart, T. (1963). *The interpretation of music.* New York: Harper & Row.

Eskelin, G. (1994). *Musical ear training improvisation charts.* Woodland Hills, CA: Stage 3.

Experiments in musical creativity. (1966). Washington, DC: MENC.

Farber, A. (1991). "Speaking the musical language." *Music Educators Journal, 78*(4), 30–34.

Ferand, E. T. (1961). *Anthology of music: Improvisation in nine centuries of western music.* Cologne: Verlag.

Garcia, A. J. (1990). "Pedagogical scat." *Music Educators Journal* 77(1), 28–34.

Gordon, E. E. (1996). *Harmonic improvisation readiness record.*

Chicago: GIA.

Greenberg, N., & Maynard, P. (1975). *An anthology of early renaissance music*. London: Norton.

Hackett, P. (1998). *The melody book* (3rd ed.). Upper Saddle River, NJ: Prentice Hall.

Hackett, P., & Lindeman, C.A. (1997). *The musical classroom* (4th ed.). Upper Saddle River, NJ: Prentice Hall.

Horsley, I., Collins, M., Badura-Skoda, E., & Libby, D. (1995). "Improvisation: Western art music." In S. Sadie (Ed.), *The new Grove dictionary of music and musicians* (Vol. 9). London: Macmillan.

Jairazbhoy, N. A. (1995). "Improvisation: Asian art music." In S. Sadie (Ed.), *The new Grove dictionary of music and musicians* (Vol. 9). London: Macmillan.

Jakfar, A. (1995). *Indonesia—Madura: Art music*. (M. Desbureaux, Trans.). Paris: Ocora—Radio France.

Johnson, R. (1981). *Scores: An anthology of new music*. New York: Schirmer.

Kaschub, M. (1997). "Exercising the musical imagination." *Music Educators Journal, 84*(3), 26–32.

Konowitz, B. (1973). *Music improvisation as a classroom method*. New York: Alfred.

Kratus, J. (1995). "A developmental approach to teaching music improvisation." *International Journal of Music Education, 26*, 27–38.

Madura, P. D. (1995). "An exploratory investigation of the assessment of vocal jazz improvisation." *Psychology of Music, 23*(1), 48–62.

Madura, P. D. (1997). "Jazz improvisation for the vocal student." *Teaching Music, 4*(6), 26–28.

Madura, P. D. (1996). "Relationships among vocal jazz improvisation achievement, jazz theory knowledge, imitative ability, musical experience, creativity, and gender." *Journal of Research in Music Education, 44*(3), 252–67.

Mark, M. (1996). *Contemporary music education* (3rd ed.). New York: Schirmer.

Marsh, M. V. (1970). *Explore and discover music*. Toronto: Macmillan.

McPherson, G. E. (1994). "Improvisation: Past present and future." In H. Lees (Ed.), *Musical connections: Tradition and change* [Proceedings of the 21st world conference of the International Society for Music Education held in Tampa, Florida], (154–62). The University of Aukland, New Zealand: Uniprint.

Mead, V. H. (1994). *Dalcroze eurhythmics in today's music classroom*.

New York: Schott.

National standards for arts education (1994). Reston, VA: MENC.

Nettl, B., Capwell, C., Bohlman, P. V., Wong, I. K. F., & Turino, T. (1992), *Excursions in world music.* Englewood Cliffs: Prentice Hall.

Opportunity-to-learn standards for music instruction: Grades PreK–12 (1994). Reston, VA: MENC.

Parker, A. (1976). *Creative hymn singing.* Chapel Hill: Hinshaw.

Robinson, R. (1977). *Choral ornamentation.* Chapel Hill: Hinshaw.

Robinson, R., & Winold, A. (1992). *The choral experience: Literature, materials, and methods.* New York: Waveland.

Sadie, S. (Ed.) (1988). *The Norton/Grove concise encyclopedia of music.* New York: Norton.

Schafer, R. M. (1988). *The thinking ear.* Toronto: Arcana.

Shaw, K. (1990). *Warm-ups for the jazz/show choir.* Greeley: University of Northern Colorado Jazz Press.

Smallwood, R. (1980). "Gospel and blues improvisation." *Music Educators Journal,* 66(5), 100–104.

"The state of the standards." (1997). *Music Educators Journal,* 5(3), 9.

Steen, A. (1992). *Exploring Orff: A teacher's guide.* New York: Schott.

Steinel, D. (1984). *Music and music education: Data and information.* Reston, VA: MENC.

Stoloff, B. (1996). *Scat! Vocal improvisation techniques.* Brooklyn: Gerard & Sarzin.

Stravinsky, I. (1942). *Poetics of Music.* Cambridge: Harvard University Press.

Suzuki, S. (1984). *Nurtured by Love.* Smithtown, NY: Exposition.

Swanwick, K., & Tillman, J. (1986). "The sequence of musical development: A study of children's composition." *British Journal of Music Education, 3* (3), 305–339.

Teaching jazz: A course of study (1996). Reston, VA: MENC & IAJE.

Thompson, K. P. (1980). "Vocal improvisation for elementary students." *Music Educators Journal,* 66(5), 69–71.

Warner, B. (1991). *Orff-Schulwerk: Applications for the classroom.* Englewood Cliffs: Prentice Hall.

Acknowledgments

The contributions of the following people helped make this publication possible:

Choralist E-mail respondents who suggested choral scores with improvisation: John Boozer, David Buley, Mari Eleanor, Mary Goetze, Neils Graesholm, Bill McConnell, Sarah Meredith, Ally Salyer, Gilbert Seeley, C. M. Shearer, Diane Trotter, and Judith Cook Tucker.

University of Southern California graduate students who contributed teaching strategies while enrolled in "Beginning Improvisation for Music Teachers" during the Spring 1998 semester: Nopanand Chanorathaikul, Jaehee Choi, Sherilene Chycoski, Susan Helfter, Younghee Lee, Susan Park, and Jennifer Sorgatz.

My Indiana University mentors who planted the seeds for many topics found within: Professors David Baker, Charles Schmidt, Jan Harrington, Mary Goetze, and the late Jean Sinor.

USC Thornton School of Music Dean Larry Livingston and Professor Jay Zorn, who provide an academic environment where creative thinking can flourish.

David Ward-Steinman: Composer-in-Residence and Professor of Music, San Diego State University, for his encyclopedic mind, megatherian library, and ardent support.

Margaret Senko: MENC Director of Publications, whose professionalism is a blessing.

This book is dedicated to my mother, Henrietta P. Madura, on her 85th birthday.

www.ingramcontent.com/pod-product-compliance
Lightning Source LLC
Chambersburg PA
CBHW071934240426
43668CB00038B/1797